Copyright © 2022 Text by Emmaly Wiederholt and Silva Laukkanen
Copyright © 2022 Images by Elizabeth C. Brent-Maldonado

All rights reserved. This book or any portion thereof may not be reproduced or used in any manner whatsoever without the express written permission of the publisher except for the use of brief quotations.

Printed in the United States of America

First Printing, 2022
ISBN 978-0-9982478-1-6

Emmaly Wiederholt
2924 Monterey Ave. SE
Albuquerque, NM 87106
stanceondance.com

Elizabeth C. Brent-Maldonado
494 27th Ave. Apt 58
San Francisco, CA 94121
www.sparkle.vision

Dancers depicted in front cover illustration are (L-R) Erik Ferguson, Christelle Dreyer, Nastija Fijolič, Toby MacNutt, Alexandria Wailes, Alice Sheppard, Evan Ruggiero, and Jerron Herman.

Breadth of Bodies
Discussing Disability in Dance

By Emmaly Wiederholt and Silva Laukkanen
Edited by Emmaly Wiederholt

Illustrations by Liz Brent-Maldonado

Breadth of Bodies
Discussing Disability in Dance

TABLE OF CONTENTS

Introduction	i
Redouan "Redo" Ait Chitt	65
Yulia Arakelyan	45
Marc Brew	129
Hai Cohen	21
Sidiki Conde	137
Hanna Cormick	101
Suzanne Cowan	81
Charlene Curtiss	69
Christelle Dreyer	29
Erik Ferguson	41
Nastija Fijolič	121
Kayla Hamilton	53
Jerron Herman	109
Antoine Hunter	37
Lusi Insiati	13
Isabel Cristina Jiménez	49

Maija Karhunen	33
Kelcie Laube	85
Laurel Lawson	105
Jung Soo "Krops" Lee	61
Kris Lenzo	25
Kitty Lunn	133
Toby MacNutt	9
Kazuyo Morita	93
Luca "Lazylegz" Patuelli	57
Mark Travis Rivera	73
Evan Ruggiero	117
Hannah Sampson	77
Bill Shannon	97
Alice Sheppard	1
Judith Smith	5
Mary Verdi-Fletcher	89
Alexandria Wailes	125
Krishna Washburn	17
Elizabeth Winkelaar	113
Collaborators Biographies	iii
Donor Thanks	iv

INTRODUCTION

By Emmaly Wiederholt, in conversation with Silva Laukkanen

One in four people in the United States has a disability that impacts a major part of their life, according to a 2018 report by the Centers for Disease Control and Prevention[1]. There are few dance environments that mirror that statistic. And because the dance world would be stronger and richer artistically if it did, my colleague Silva Laukkanen and I have compiled these interviews that seek to document the lived experience of the dancers who are making that shift happen.

I began this project after choreographer Alice Sheppard invited me to see her touring piece *DESCENT* in 2017. I was unable to do so but instead suggested an interview with her for my publication Stance on Dance. I had known Alice from my experience performing with AXIS Dance Company in 2009. Alice had since become an independent dance artist, and I was intrigued to learn more about her journey creating a piece that was specifically choreographed for two women using wheelchairs.

After the interview, Alice informally shared with me her general frustration with the press. From her years of experience working in AXIS Dance Company and then as an independent dance artist, she recognized a pattern in which reviewers, dance writers, and scholars in dance and performance studies tend to focus more on disability when writing about disabled dance artists, rather than on their art. I thought this was an intriguing phenomenon to dive into.

In 2017, I published my first book, *Beauty is Experience: Dancing 50 and Beyond*, in which I interviewed dancers ranging in age from 50 to 95. By focusing specifically on aging in dance, I was beginning to have more awareness of access and representation. However, the book was generally inspirational. Here, Alice was proposing a different narrative: Where is the inspiration coming from – the fact that the aging (or in this case disabled) person is dancing, or because of what they artistically have to say?

My friend Silva is a passionate advocate for dancers with disabilities and has taught extensively in integrated dance. For the past few years, she has also been producing the podcast, DanceCast. My intuition in asking Silva to join me in this budding project was her considerable connections within the disability dance community. I also reached out to Liz Brent-Maldonado, a good friend and talented visual artist in San Francisco, to create original illustrations. Liz previously illustrated for Stance on Dance, and I've always admired her ability to blend realism and whimsy.

Our interview questions focus not only on each dancer's history and practice, but also their experience navigating stereotypes, press, educational opportunities, language preferences, and assimilation. Because our questions demand an intimate knowledge of the dance world, the focus of our project became professional dance artists with a significant amount of experience. Though there is great work being done in educational settings for dancers with disabilities, our aim was interviewing those with substantial performance experience. Since teaching and performing are often parallel trajectories in the arts, many of our interviewees have extensive teaching experience as well, but they were selected to be interviewed because of their experience working as dance artists.

Silva and I are aware that the word "disability" does not encompass one experience, and thus tried to include dance artists with different disabilities including those who use a wheelchair, use crutches, are Deaf, are visually impaired, or have an intellectual disability. We additionally reached out to dance artists from various genres and diverse racial and gender identities.

Our selection of interviewees thus reflects larger conversations on racial and gender representation, as well as conversations about access not only in terms of ramps and interpreters, but also socio-economic and geographic access to attend dance classes and performances. There have been many intersections to keep in mind during this project. In the end, Silva and I interviewed 35 professional dancers with disabilities from 15 countries who practice a variety of dance forms and who comprise multiple identities.

This is not a "who's who" or compilation of all the dancers with disabilities. Instead, it's a cross-section. As our subtitle suggests, it's meant to be a discussion of disability in dance. As we neared completion, Silva and I were fueled by the depth and variety of disability dance artistry around the world; there are infinitely more dancers than we could realistically include, and we sincerely hope someone picks up where we left off.

Finally, we want to acknowledge that Silva and I are not disabled and come from places of privilege. We are attempting to use that privilege to host a dialogue we believe should be happening in dance.

What exactly is that dialogue? If dance is art, and art is expression, and expression is predicated on experience, shouldn't we seek a breadth of experiences? Most dance environments are rather homogenous in terms of types of bodies in the room. The intersection of dance and disability feels like the perfect place to tackle this. Dance is "of-the-body" by definition (meaning it doesn't depend on an instrument, paintbrush, or camera). An art form that acknowledges the reality of the body and its many manifestations might be more successful in saying something that honestly and profoundly reflects how we live.

We hope this book provides the opportunity to give some thought as to what makes art inspirational, what makes technique beautiful, and what assumptions are commonly made about dancers' bodies. What would the dance world be like if it acknowledged, embraced, and celebrated having at least 25 percent of its population be dancers with disabilities?

---

1 "CDC: 1 in 4 US adults live with a disability," Press release dated Thursday, August 16, 2018, <https://www.cdc.gov/media/releases/2018/p0816-disability.html>

Alice Sheppard

After taking her first dance class on a dare, **Alice Sheppard** *resigned her academic professorship to pursue dance. As a member of AXIS Dance Company, she toured nationally and taught in the company's outreach programs. Since becoming an independent artist, Alice has danced with Marjani Forté, MBDance, Infinity Dance Theater, Steve Paxton, Full Radius Dance Company, and MOMENTA Dance Company, and has been commissioned by CRIPSiE, Full Radius Dance Company, and MOMENTA Dance Company. She is the founder and artistic director of Kinetic Light.*

"I Want to Build a Network of Legacy"

This interview was conducted by Emmaly Wiederholt in May 2018

How did you get into dance and what have been some highlights in your dance history?

I earned a doctorate in Medieval Studies at Cornell University and then taught English and Comparative Literature at Pennsylvania State University. In 2004, after a conference on disability studies, I took on a dare from disabled dancer Homer Avila to take a dance class. I loved it and took the AXIS Dance Company summer intensive workshop. The first lessons I took in ballet and wheelchair technique were taught by Kitty Lunn of Infinity Dance Theater. My first performance was with Kitty at the Joyce Soho. From there, I continued lessons with AXIS Dance Company, became an apprentice in 2006, and became a company member in 2007. I toured with the company nationally and taught in their education and outreach programs.

In 2012, I became an independent dancer and choreographer and have since worked with companies in the United Kingdom and the United States. A couple years ago, I initiated Kinetic Light, a collaboration with dancer Laurel Lawson and lighting/video artist Michael Maag. Michael, Laurel, and I toured *DESCENT,* our first evening-length work, choreographed by me in collaboration with Laurel, featuring an architectural ramp that acts as a partner in the choreography and storytelling. The ramp was designed by Sara Hendren, Yevgeniya Zastavker, and students at Olin College.

The history of disability and dance in the US goes back a long way, but the dance world does not know it. I want to build a network of legacy by naming the disabled dancers who have influenced me: Stephanie Bastos, Rodney Bell, Marc Brew, Laurel Lawson, Bonnie Lewkowicz, Kitty Lunn, and Judith Smith. Because of the relative newness of the field and the subsequent deficit of training and educational opportunities, most of my developmental thinking comes from a cross-disciplinary approach, including disability scholars and artists Eli Clare, Rosemarie Garland-Thomson, Georgina Kleege, Riva Lehrer, Simi Linton, and Tobin Siebers. These people have shaped not only how I think about movement, but how I understand the value of disability in the creative process.

How would you describe your current dance practice?

My dance practice involves a lot of research and thinking about the culture of disability. I look at other works being done by disabled culture-makers. My movement practices are scattered at this point. I take mainstream modern dance class and the occasional ballet class. I also swim, go to the gym for strength training, and do yoga.

My movement practice is also rooted in my relationship to technologies, and not just technologies that I use like my wheelchair or crutches, but also technologies around us. I mix mainstream dance vocabularies, the identity of impairment, and the relationship of disability arts and culture to technology.

When you tell people you are a dancer, what are the most common reactions you receive?

If it's non-disabled people in the non-dance world, I tell people that I use my wheelchair to be a dancer, or I say that I'm a disabled dancer who uses a wheelchair. By putting my disability front and center, I immediately get around whatever people's expectations are.

If I'm lucky, they'll say, "Oh, like AXIS." And I'll reply that yes, I was an AXIS dancer for five or six years, and I'm making my own work now. The only thing many people may have heard of with regards to disability dance is AXIS. I'm proud to have been with AXIS, but I'm making my own career now, and I'm my own artist.

The United States has not yet nourished its independent disabled artists. There's a strong repertory company scene that's developing, but there's not a strong scene of disabled independent artists. The UK is ahead of the US in that regard. It's a question of funding. Individual disabled artists can get funded to make work at a professional level there.

> "The history of disability and dance in the US goes back a long way, but the dance world does not know it. I want to build a network of legacy by naming the disabled dancers who have influenced me.

What are some ways people discuss dance with regards to disability that you feel carry problematic implications or assumptions?

Most dance writers are not literate in wheeled, crutch, or disabled movement. And many are not familiar with the work of other companies and artists in the field. This means that they have less context for evaluating the choreography and the dancers, so they end up relying on what they know about other dance techniques. This is why they often respond to what is visually spectacular. They project what they imagine someone with a disability should or shouldn't be able to do. It gets to the point where we're not really talking about the movement on the dancers' bodies; we're talking about the writer's uneducated perspective on disability movement.

Part of the difficulty is that we're dealing with societal imaginations of disability as a lack of ability. Disability as identity, culture, politics, and aesthetic are not as familiar to people outside the disability arts world. So people turn to what they know: disability as a lack of ability. Because of this, critical writers often don't recognize or understand the traditions and training behind the choreography. They don't have the cultural wallpaper. They lack cross references, and thus are unable to detect patterns of influence, innovation, or work that references other works.

Use the internet. See other pieces. Look at work samples. Read other reviews. Find out what the appropriate language is. I once read an article where an African dance choreographer challenged one of the New York Times writers on the notion of ignorance. The choreographer said something in response to a review along the lines of, "You may say that this piece wasn't innovative, but you're not familiar with the fundamental African forms that would enable you to recognize innovation."

I know that everyone has no time and is over committed, but I would recommend writers be up to date on disability language and culture as much as possible.

Do you believe there are adequate training opportunities for dancers with disabilities? If not, what areas would you specifically like to see improved?

Of course not. Here's what I envision: First, I want dancers with disabilities to be able to get training like any other dancer. That includes training in the major techniques and somatic practices, as well as the history and notable works. I want people to be able to have coursework on physically integrated dance and study work by disabled artists. There's no reason that education in the field of dance and dance history shouldn't be made available to disabled dancers.

Second, I want dancers to be able to be trained in the movement expressions and cultures of their own impairment. If you go to a mainstream dance class, the teacher probably won't teach you how to use a wheelchair, but there is technique to using crutches or a wheelchair. There are also techniques to figuring out what blindness brings to dance. Deaf dance is its own art form. Right now, most disabled dance artists end up figuring most things out for themselves, but there are specific principles that can be shared among people who have the same impairment.

Finally, I want every dance teacher at the university level to be trained to teach physically integrated dance and disability dance. Disabled dancers should be able to go to a conservatory or get a BFA or MFA. Teachers should be versed in disability scholarship and be contributing to that scholarship.

Would you like to see disability in dance assimilated into the mainstream?

That's like saying to an African American choreographer, "Should dance be whitened?" We must recognize that physically integrated dance is an art form in its own right. We wouldn't try to "assimilate" ballet, modern, or hip hop. An art form deserves its own place in the field. Then, the question of assimilation goes away. Art forms need to be supported rather than mainstreamed. The pressure on a disabled person is already to join the mainstream and erase the disability.

What is your preferred term for the field?

I like being called "disabled artist." "Physically integrated dance" is the accepted term in the US for the work being done by companies like AXIS, Full Radius Dance, and Dancing Wheels. Terms like "mixed abilities" get away from the art form and look at the abilities of the dancers instead. The term sets us back by focusing on ability instead of art. As Judith Smith used to say, "It makes you wonder about the mixed abilities; who are the good dancers, and who are the bad dancers?"

The thing about "differently abled" is that, just because I use a wheelchair, I don't have different abilities than others. I don't have a superpower, for example. I understand that people who use terms like "differently abled" use them because of the stigma that's often attached societally to disability as being a deficit of diagnosis. But disability is not a deficit of diagnosis. It's a political term; it's a term of art and culture, a term of pride and identity, a term used by scholars, artists, and activists. When you add this context and set of meanings, it changes everything.

In your perspective, is the field improving with time?

This conversation wouldn't have been happening five years ago. There's more awareness now. The field is growing. People are taking greater risks. I'm excited.

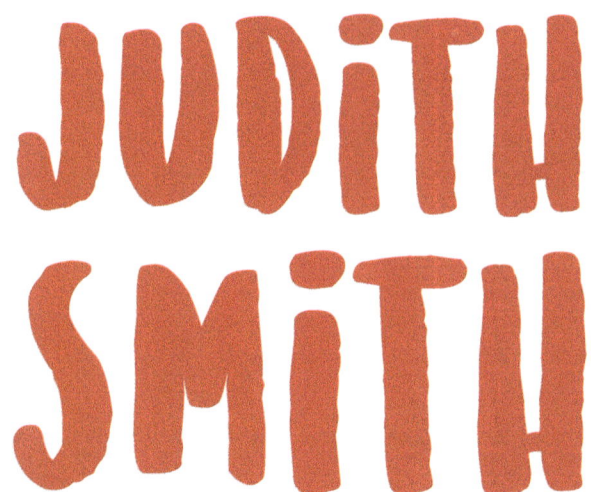

Judith Smith, *founding member and artistic director emerita of AXIS Dance Company, is a driving force in physically integrated dance. She helped launch AXIS in 1987 and grew the company to be a leading physically integrated dance ensemble. Under Judith's artistic direction from 1997 to 2017, AXIS commissioned more than 35 works from choreographers and composers nationwide, toured to more than 100 cities, appeared twice on FOX TV'S* So You Think You Can Dance, *and developed extensive education/outreach programs. In 2016, her advocacy led to the first National Convening on the Future of Physically Integrated Dance in the US.*

"Making Physically Integrated Work Part of The Dance Canon"

This interview was conducted by Emmaly Wiederholt in February 2020

How did you get into dance and what have been some highlights in your dance history?

I moved from Colorado to Berkeley in 1983, five years into my disability, and met an attendant who was also an improviser. We started doing improvisational movement, and it changed my life.

When I became disabled, I had been a champion equestrian. Everything I did was body focused. After I got hurt, I felt alienated from myself and from society. I spent a lot of time sitting still not knowing what to do in my body. When I started doing improvisational movement, it gave me an avenue to reconnect with being physical and to find ways to move that were enjoyable and exploratory. For me, it had direct implications on my quality of life in terms of gaining independence, strength, balance, coordination, and confidence.

From there, I ended up in a self-defense class for women with disabilities in Oakland. I met another student in the class who was not disabled, Thais Mazur, and who was a martial arts and dance practitioner. She asked if I wanted to be in a dance piece for Dance Brigade's Furious Feet Festival for Social Change. The closest I'd ever gotten to dance was dressage on horses, but I was intrigued enough to say yes. I got hooked. I knew we were doing something that hadn't been done. There was a fair amount of contact improvisation for people with and without disabilities, but we didn't know anybody setting choreography. This was 1987. It was exciting to move in different ways by myself and with other people. Having non-disabled partners opened new possibilities.

We needed a name for our group, and we wanted something that didn't directly say "wheelchair," though we wanted to acknowledge it. We came up with the name "Axis," though it went through a lot of iterations over the years before it became AXIS Dance Company. The axis of a wheel ended up being a beautiful metaphor.

After that first performance, the disabled community got interested in what we were doing, and as a result we were asked to make pieces for various disability events. Then the dance community became interested. We kept getting offers to make work. At the same time, people wanted to learn about what we were doing, so we started our education program with a monthly jam right out the gate.

A lot happened between how things started and when I retired. By the end, I stopped performing in new work because I'd injured my shoulder and couldn't do 80-hour weeks anymore. Besides being in the studio 20 to 30 hours a week, I still had 50 to 60 hours a week of admin to do. I knew I wanted the company to continue and grow, so I chose to focus on the administrative work. I think I was successful in developing great programs, and I managed to raise money and find foundational support, but it exhausted me. So I made the decision a few years ago to retire.

How would you describe your current dance practice?

I do improvisational movement on my own. It's a meditation practice. I also do vigorous aerobic movement because I like to work out. I keep thinking I'm going to get back to dance jams, but I haven't yet. In the summer of 2019, I was in a dance film that Carina Ho directed and choreographed. That was a lot of fun. It featured five of us who use power chairs.

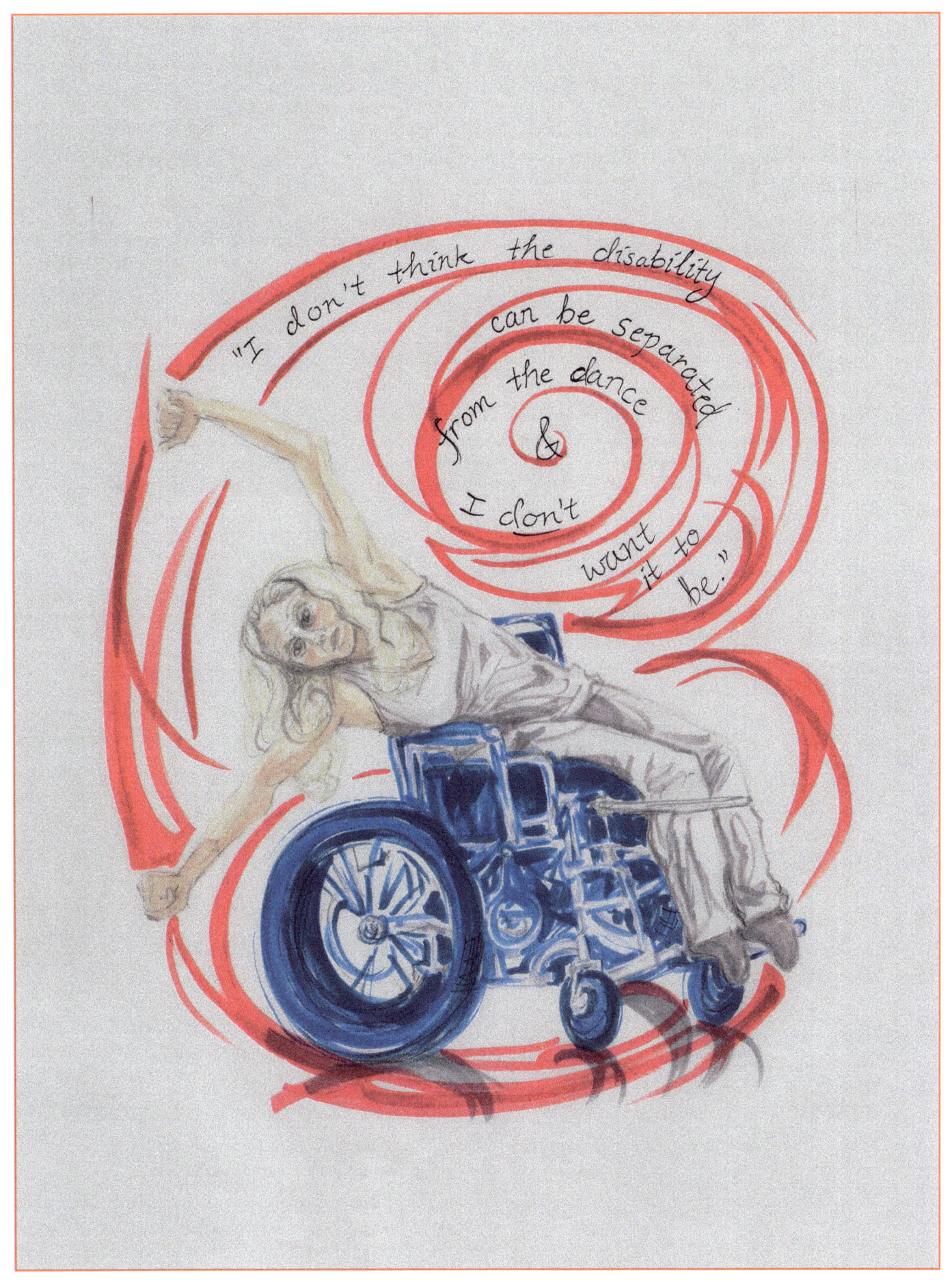

When you tell people you are a dancer, what are the most common reactions you receive?

Laughing is one. Another reaction is a blank stare, like they're not able to register my meaning. I think the funniest is, "Oh you can walk?" People find it very difficult to put dance together with the picture of someone as disabled as I am. It's a paradox to most people.

What are some ways people discuss dance with regards to disability that you feel carry problematic implications or assumptions?

We spent the first 10 years trying to convince funders, critics, and presenters that we were doing dance, not therapy. Especially early on, a lot of the writing about us was along the lines of, "Isn't it wonderful what these people are doing?" They would write about the disability and not focus on the work.

That being said, a lot of our early work was directly about disability. The company went through an implosion 10 years in. One of the things that triggered it was a poor review about a performance we did in Minneapolis in 1995. This was also the first time I thought we got a serious review, and I agreed with it. The reviewer said the dancers were strong, but the choreography was sophomore. Thais was not happy about that. I wanted to dissect the review as a company and figure out how to move the artistic work forward, and that's what led to the implosion.

At that point, I ended up taking the responsibility of making sure AXIS continued. A big part of what those of us who remained wanted was to stop doing pieces directly about disability. I was one of the people who wanted to start commissioning other choreographers to work with us. I was bored stiff of what we were coming up with. When you're disabled, you don't have the opportunity to drop into any dance class. I felt that the way to get new inspiration was to commission choreographers. That's when the writing about us changed.

The first repertoire I commissioned was Bill T. Jones, Joe Goode, Joanna Haigood, and Sonya Delwaide. Reviewers had a context within which to review the work because they knew those choreographers' other works. It gave them a different lens.

I started AXIS' commissioning program out of selfishness. I wanted new motivation and I wanted to be pushed. It ended up being a successful strategy on all levels. People took us seriously. It gave us a way into funders we didn't have before because people were interested to see what well-known choreographers would do with us. On the inside, it was so invigorating to be in the studio with different choreographers. And the writing about us reflected all that.

What happens for a lot of people when they first see this work is that it is hard for them not to focus on the disability. I don't think the disability can be separated from the dance, and I don't want it to be. But what I would suggest for someone getting into writing about integrated/inclusive dance is to educate themselves: Are you writing from the lens of amazement that a disabled person can get out of bed, or are you writing from a lens of evaluating the technique and choreography?

> "AXIS undertook a huge task in 1998 when we started commissioning work by contemporary choreographers and making physically integrated work part of the dance canon.

Do you believe there are adequate training opportunities for dancers with disabilities? If not, what areas would you specifically like to see improved?

No, there are not. In 2014, the managing director that AXIS brought in asked what I hadn't done that I wanted to do. I responded that the field needs to be organized.

Jeremy Alliger, founder of Dance Umbrella, was a huge part of developing integrated dance in the US. In 1996, he approached AXIS about doing a festival, which Thais and I helped plan and curate with Jeremy. The first International Festival of Wheelchair Dance brought together 14 companies from around the country and world in 1997. But in 2014 the field hadn't gotten together since then.

I wanted to do a national convening that focused on where the field was and where it needed to be. I especially wanted to compare it to what was happening in the UK and Europe. I felt like we were behind, particularly in comparison to the UK.

We did a national convening in New York City in 2016. I had planned on 25 people attending, but we ended up with more than 50 and a nice cross section of the field, from choreographers to dance artists, funders, presenters, dance writers, and artistic directors. It also represented three generations of integrated dance. It was a pivotal moment. What was exciting about the national convening was that Dance/USA was our media partner. There is now a Dance/USA Deaf & Disability Affinity Group, which I co-chair.

The national convening was followed by six regional convenings around the country in 2016. I wanted to address why the artistic quality of our field was not where it needed to be after 30 years and what we could do about it. We came up with needing training and opportunities for disabled dancers and choreographers.

Out of that, AXIS created the AXIS Artistic Advancement Platform. It's one of the things I'm most proud of. The platform addresses opportunities to train teachers, dancers, and choreographers at all entry points, from kids through the university level. It's an ambitious program. We were able to get major funding from Mellon, Ford, and Duke. It ignited this drive to organize and move the field forward.

Would you like to see disability in dance assimilated into the mainstream?

There are already disabled dancers who are graduating with dance degrees, like Julie Crothers, Lani Dickinson, and Stephanie Bastos, but they are all amputees. The more disabled you are, the harder it is to integrate. It's not that it was easy for Julie, Stephanie, and Lani; they definitely worked harder than others to be taken seriously. But for someone in a wheelchair, it's even harder. I know fewer wheelchair users who have gotten dance degrees, and the ones I do know were able to because someone on faculty got behind them.

It's important to have companies like Alice Sheppard's Kinetic Light that are focused just on disabled artists. I personally was more excited by integrated work than I would have been only working with other disabled artists, but both are important and greatly inform each other.

What is your preferred term for the field?

I don't like "mixed abilities" because it infers that some of the dancers are good and some suck. We stopped using that term years ago. I like "inclusive dance." "Physically integrated dance" is what I used with AXIS because it best described what we were doing. In the performance company, we didn't have developmentally disabled dancers.

Until the ADA *[Americans with Disabilities Act]*, nobody was asking about disability on grant applications. I would take a red pen and write "disabled" underneath the other demographic information, which was usually asking about gender and race. It took the passing of the ADA for disability to even get on grant proposals.

In your perspective, is the field improving with time?

Well yeah. But in 2014, 30 years in, I was still disappointed in the level of artistry and opportunities available. Since 2016, the work Dance/NYC has done and the national and regional convenings AXIS undertook have been pivotal. The opportunities have increased exponentially as a result.

Any other thoughts?

There are things I wanted to accomplish that I didn't, but AXIS undertook a huge task in 1998 when we started commissioning work by contemporary choreographers and making physically integrated work part of the dance canon. I feel great we were able to accomplish that.

TOBY MACNUTT

"It's Both And"

This interview was conducted by Emmaly Wiederholt in June 2018

Toby MacNutt *is a queer, nonbinary-trans, disabled multidisciplinary artist, author, and teacher based in Vermont. Toby's training and experience includes a wide breadth of contemporary, improvisational, and adaptive styles, with a childhood foundation in ballet, jazz, and modern dance. They have studied with integrated companies such as AXIS, Stopgap, and Candoco, as well as with individual teachers, choreographers, and experienced performance mentors. Their performance history ranges from yoga studios in small Vermont towns to Danspace at St. Mark's in New York City to festivals in the UK and Germany.*

How did you get into dance and what have been some highlights in your dance history?

I started dance when I was five. I did ballet, modern, and jazz until high school. My disability started to make itself known in my early teenage years when I hit puberty. No one knew what was going on, so it was assumed dance was injurious, and I had to stop when I was 13 or 14. I went from dancing a couple hours a day to nothing at all, and it was heartbreaking.

It took almost a decade for my diagnosis to get straightened out. I was also in a different place mentally, physically, and geographically. I started to come to terms with the idea that "disabled" was a label that applied to me and that it wasn't all that bad. I saw AXIS Dance Company perform and met disabled dancer/choreographer Alice Sheppard. Around that time, my good friend Becca gave me a pep talk, saying, "Once a dancer, always a dancer. Of course you can still dance."

So I started dancing again, which was wonderful. It had been such heartbreak for so many years. I hadn't been able to bring myself to go see dance, and suddenly I was dancing. I got snatched up by Heidi Latsky who was touring *The GIMP Project* at the time. It came through my town, I went and did the workshops, and Heidi asked if I wanted to go to New York and work with the project. I said, "Yes, sure, that sounds great!" That catapulted me back in.

I worked with Heidi for a while, as well as with some local choreographers in Vermont. When I could, I traveled to take classes and workshops with other companies. That was really valuable, particularly working with AXIS in their summer lab. I also spent a little time studying with Candoco and Stopgap in the UK.

However, being a choreographer wasn't something I had the confidence to do. While working with Tiffany Rhynard, who put together a project in Vermont called *Subverting Normal*, I realized I had choreographed everything I was performing as well as some parts that other dancers were performing. Apparently I had become a choreographer.

I got my first grant shortly after and started making work. I presented my first evening length work, *One, Two*, on a mixed-ability cast of six in 2014.

How would you describe your current dance practice?

For many years, swimming has been my ongoing exercise. At this time, I have a puppy who is a year and a half old. Exercising him – he's a German Shepherd – is a substantial part of my fitness regimen. I also started aerial silks about two years ago, which is a phenomenal workout. I'm just getting to the point where I have enough skill to start building choreography with it.

I don't take conventional modern dance classes very often. Those classes are often frustrating because I have to spend a lot of time just adapting the material rather than developing the underlying technique skills. I try to take classes from instructors who can help me with that process so I can develop technique, not just build my skill adapting. I also make work, though not with the frequency I'd prefer. I just premiered a new installation piece. It was a bit experimental for Vermont, but most of the audience seemed to have a profound response. I also performed a solo at the Fresh Meat Festival this year in San Francisco.

When you tell people you are a dancer, what are the most common reactions you receive?

They've changed over the years. Initially, I experienced a paternalistic response: "That's so nice for you." People didn't grasp that my dancing could have a professional quality. I don't get that as much now. It's hard to say whether that's evidence of a cultural shift and people are more aware of the fact that dance is available to disabled people, or if it's an effect of who I am and who I interact with. I've undergone a gender transition, and people often read me more seriously now that I am perceived as male. But it may also be that I have more confidence and sound more professional.

What are some ways people discuss dance with regards to disability that you feel carry problematic implications or assumptions?

All the inspiration shit. The blanket statement "you're so inspirational" frustrates the heck out of me. I don't mind being inspiring for my art, but I do mind being inspiring simply for existing. That's not the bar I'm looking to clear. The other thing that irritates me is when someone says, "I stopped seeing your disability." If you're not seeing my disability, you have missed a serious component of my work and how it is supposed to be seen.

At least once per show, someone will come up to me and say, "You don't really need those crutches; look at you, you're so strong and graceful," as if I'm supposed to fake being non-disabled. People don't seem to be able to reconcile that I can be fast, strong, and graceful, and still genuinely need mobility assistance.

Learn what the stereotypes are. You can't avoid them if you aren't familiar with them. Learn about the community and the ways we talk about ourselves. Learn how varied those responses can be; what might offend one person will be the preferred term for someone else.

Once you have that knowledge under your belt, engage with the dance as dance, rather than as a cultural metaphor. Look at the movement and the lighting or staging choices before interpreting the work. Don't interpret before observing.

> "I'm going to take my classic non-binary fluidly disabled approach and say, 'It's both and.' I definitely would like to see less of a gulf between disabled dance-making and non-disabled/mainstream dance-making... However, it's not entirely up to us if we integrate more.

Do you believe there are adequate training opportunities for dancers with disabilities? If not, what areas would you specifically like to see improved?

There are several levels to that problem that need to be addressed. There's the basic problem that instructional staff aren't prepared to teach us. It's so rare to find a teacher who can actually help me with my technique. It's a teachable skill set, but it's not something non-disabled dance teachers learn. How do you teach someone whose body or brain works radically different than yours? It is do-able, but it's a skill that is underdeveloped.

Then there are several problematic structural elements. For instance, when there are classes for disabled dancers, they tend to be clustered in big cities. For dancers like me who live outside big cities, how do we get people to understand dance can be an option for them?

We do have more models now in terms of the opportunity to see a performance and think, "Maybe I could do that." The internet has helped there. But we still have ground to cover. Workshops and labs are really wonderful, but they are often expensive and far away. How do we make those opportunities more accessible?

Would you like to see disability in dance assimilated into the mainstream?

I'm going to take my classic non-binary fluidly disabled approach and say, "It's both and." I definitely would like to see less of a gulf between disabled dance-making and non-disabled/mainstream dance-making. Integration is important, both socially and artistically.

The field can only benefit in terms of getting more opportunities and getting theaters to upgrade their accessibility. However, it's not entirely up to us if we integrate more.

At the same time, the affinity spaces and disability-focused dance spaces are so valuable in that we aren't coming from the same aesthetic position or understanding of movement, beauty, or the body that mainstream non-disabled dance is. I don't want to lose that context for our work. I don't want to lose the chance to make work on bodies like ours, instead of having once again to adjust for non-disabled bodies and brains. I want to see that richness and dive in. I want to make work by us and for us, and then perhaps people who aren't us will be able to connect, but without us reshaping ourselves into the mainstream mold.

You can have normalization without integration. That's on the side of theaters and getting them to recognize that disabled dance is its own valid discipline, even though we don't share one aesthetic or technique. Audiences can be excited by our work without it becoming in line with non-disabled dance traditions.

What is your preferred term for the field?

I most frequently use "disabled dance" and "adaptive dance." "Inclusive" doesn't feel like it connotes equal professional footing. "Adaptive" sort of has those implications so I use it, for example, when I take a master class that isn't designed for me. If a group of mixed disabled and non-disabled dancers are learning the same work from a non-disabled choreographer, I would describe that as "adaptive" because it's a description of the adaption involved in the process. When talking about my own work, choreographed by a disabled person on disabled dancers, then I use "disabled dance" or "disability dance." And personally, I prefer "disabled dancer."

I don't know if there's ever going to be a perfect term because we're not monolithic. We come from different cultural and dance backgrounds, and have different bodily and social experiences with disability. But we do need a term to describe where we sit in relation to mainstream non-disabled dance and for me, that term is "disability dance."

In your perspective, is the field improving with time?

That's another "both and." It's a big field with many components, from artistic quality to quantity of training opportunities to venue availability to funding. Some of these components get better and some get worse or stay the same. We're definitely seeing more in terms of dance-making, interest, and people involved. That's exciting and promising. The more we are, the more diverse we can become, the less we have to be individual silos or monoliths. We can have variety within the field if there are enough of us. None of us have to be the one true representative of the community. We can have room for our different artistic expressions.

Any other thoughts?

With regards to learning the skills required to be a choreographer, you start to develop those skills naturally when doing adaptation. But being able to have a vision of a work, translate it from your body to your dancers' bodies, and then refine it, in addition to presentation and promotion, is challenging. It's the sort of thing non-disabled dancers often learn in college. Those programs are inaccessible, both because they are often simply not open to students with disabilities, and because they are far away and expensive. Getting to practice and refine choreography is even harder. In Vermont, I don't have access to disabled dancers. In my first piece, *One, Two*, part of my time was spent just growing movement and performance skills with my dancers with less experience. I'm happy to develop those skills as a way of enriching my community, but it means I don't have as much time to experiment choreographically.

LUSI INSIATI

Lusi Insiati *is a member of Nalitari Dance Troupe. She joined Nalitari, the only inclusive dance organization in Yogyakarta, Indonesia, when it was first established in 2013. Initially an art spectator and enthusiast, she became actively involved in dance after attending Nalitari's very first workshop. Lusi continues to dance with Nalitari and has appeared in several performances, both in and out of Yogyakarta. She passionately continues expressing herself in art as an effort to increase public awareness of a more inclusive society.*

"To Be Accepted as We Are"

This interview was conducted by Silva Laukkanen in August 2020
It was translated by Yoana Wida Kristiawati

How did you get into dance and what have been some highlights in your dance history?

Initially, I was just an art enthusiast. I've always liked things related to art. When I saw my niece learning and practicing Balinese dance, I thought it would be fun to be able to dance.

I joined a pantomime group in March 2013. The pantomime event was for the anniversary of the city of Yogyakarta. Many organizations and communities were invited to perform, including a disability organization that I was part of that put on the pantomime performance. That same year, a friend from the pantomime group invited me to join Nalitari's dance workshop. I've been dancing there since.

Every performance is a highlight. I had the chance to join a two-week workshop with Introdans from the Netherlands in 2014, and the last day we held a performance together. The experience was quite new for me at the time. I was excited to be selected to represent Nalitari in the collaboration. The dance foundation in Indonesia is traditional, but the dance foundation at Introdans was ballet. I was shocked. All the workshop participants learned a little about each other's dance forms, and after that we created a collaborative dance that everyone could do. We weren't forced to master anything, but instead used the knowledge to explore what we could do. The theme was "move!"

Once, Nalitari danced in the center of Yogyakarta under hard rain. It was terribly cold and my teeth were clenching, but that was okay. None of us called it quits. We kept dancing in the rain.

One piece I especially loved was called *Circle of Life*. The dance represented the circle of life from birth to death. We explored movement on that theme.

How would you describe your current dance practice?

At Nalitari, the teaching and practice method is adjusted to people with disabilities. Any movements we can do, that is what we do. At rehearsal, we don't make a distinction between the people with and without disabilities. All the movements depend on interpretation.

Once we enter the repertoire, we learn what the dance is about so the dancers can learn how to express the idea. After that, there's a part of the dance where dancers can explore the idea by ourselves and a part where there is a guideline for movement, but it doesn't have to look the same.

We practice twice a month with all the members of Nalitari, but if there's an upcoming performance, we add more practices. There are about 30 people involved with Nalitari.

During the pandemic, we haven't had any practice. I haven't been able to see my friends, but I practice at home.

When you tell people you are a dancer, what are the most common reactions you receive?

First they are surprised. Sometimes they'll ask a question like, "How can it be?" or "What kind of dance do you do?" Then I answer by saying that I move the body parts that I can move. I always take the time to explain.

" To be really inclusive, it has to be more than that. It has to mean everyone "

When collaborating with non-disabled people, there are always challenges. In the beginning, they might feel afraid to get close or they act awkwardly. But as time passes, people adjust and it automatically feels easier to get closer or communicate. We build understanding.

In Indonesia, inclusive dance is starting to happen more, but it's not common. Sometimes other dance organizations invite disabled people to participate in a workshop, but they're not like Nalitari. We dance inclusively all the time.

What are some ways people discuss dance with regards to disability that you feel carry problematic implications or assumptions?

Most of the time, comments from people who come to see our performances are positive and encouraging. They want to learn and see more. They want to know how we practice.

The concept of inclusive dance is not common in Indonesia. When we perform, people see us as a disability organization, and the way they write about us is that we're amazing and great just because we work with people with disabilities. The comments are never about the art. Also, the non-disabled dancers are written about as supporting the disabled dancers, when in fact it is a collaboration. We work together side by side. We raise each other.

My dream is that all my disability friends can one day access dance, and that our performances are of good enough quality to be exhibited. I don't want people to come to our show because they have pity, but because the dancing is good quality.

> "My dream is for my disability friends to *access any type of dance* and that we can be accepted as we are.

Do you believe there are adequate training opportunities for dancers with disabilities? If not, what areas would you specifically like to see improved?

Not yet, but if there's someone who wants to do that, then why not?

There is also a limitation for people with disabilities to access traditional dance forms, but at Nalitari, we do not have those limitations because we do contemporary. Traditional dance is very strong here, especially in Yogyakarta. We have very strict standards. Even non-disabled people can't do certain traditional dances because of their body shape. It's a very strict culture. If you do traditional dance, you're called a "dancer."

For people with disabilities to follow all the rules of traditional dance is very difficult, but if institutions or universities start to understand that people have their own uniqueness, then perhaps things will one day change.

Here, we have a special school where all the children with disabilities go. We call it the Extraordinary School. Every region of Indonesia has at least one. Dance training would be especially great in those schools. They sometimes offer dance classes when there's an upcoming competition or performance, but it's not regular.

Nalitari has a yearly exhibition and we usually invite the teachers and students from the Extraordinary School for a workshop with us. I am one of the mentors for those workshops.

Would you like to see disability in dance assimilated into the mainstream?

We already are in Nalitari, because non-disabled and disabled people dance together. Outside Nalitari, one of my relatives is a dancer and is interested in dancing together with me. Regardless of disability, there is willingness. But up until now, it's only willingness, not action. I believe that in the future there will be action, but not in the near future.

Typically, the challenges are with the stage or performance venue, that it is too high or there is no ramp. As a wheelchair user, sometimes I become a bother for people who have to carry me and my wheelchair.

What is your preferred term for the field?

In Yogyakarta, we use "inclusive dance." But we still have people who think "inclusive" means only people with disabilities. They also think it means we only include one type of disability, like Deaf. To be really inclusive, it has to be more than that. It has to mean everyone. Nalitari has people who have physical disabilities, Down syndrome, Deafness, autism, and cerebral palsy. We only haven't worked with blind people and people with mental disorders. But if they want to join, they are welcome.

In your perspective, is the field improving with time?

Many people with disabilities are starting to come out and their voices are being heard. This is clear in the number of invitations Nalitari has received to perform. When Nalitari started, mostly just the part of the government who works with disabled people would invite us to perform. Now, non-disability related organizations are starting to invite us. Nalitari was invited to perform in a mainstream dance festival a few years ago between Indonesia, Japan, and Korea. We were the only inclusive company to perform. It was a big honor for us to bring inclusive dance to an international stage.

My dream is for my disability friends to access any type of dance and that we can be accepted as we are.

KRISHNA WASHBURN

Krishna Christine Washburn *has performed with many dance companies including Infinity Dance Theater, jill sigman/thinkdance, Heidi Latsky Dance, marked dance project, and LEIMAY. She has collaborated with several independent choreographers, including Patrice Miller, iele paloumpis, Perel, Vangeline, Micaela Mamede, Apollonia Holzer and, most notably, with A I Merino, who created Krishna's signature role as Elizabeth Bathory in* Erzsébet. *She boasts myriad ongoing artistic collaborations, including work with wearables artist Ntilit (Natalia Roumelioti). Krishna is the artistic director of The Dark Room, a multi-disciplinary project with fellow visually impaired dancer Kayla Hamilton.*

"I'm Cutthroat; This is My Career"
This interview was conducted by Emmaly Wiederholt in September 2019

How did you get into dance and what have been some highlights in your dance history?

I started dancing as a sighted child at age three. I studied ballet through the Royal Academy of Dance. I was accepted to Barnard College at age 18 and was in a preprofessional dance track. By the end of my first year, I experienced rapid dramatic vision loss. I stopped dancing for a long time. I missed dance a lot, but I didn't have any life skills; I didn't know how to walk or open a door. I was helpless for a long time. Seven years ago, I felt like I had regained confidence enough to study dance again, and I've been working professionally for five years now.

I have been a principal dancer with Infinity Dance Theater and jill sigman/thinkdance. I just did my second leading role as Elizabeth Bathory in A I Merino's *Erzsébet* at the New York Theater Festival Summerfest. I'm also working with other visually impaired dancers and choreographers like Kayla Hamilton. I used to dance for Heidi Latsky, for which people probably know me best because she uses photos of me in promo material. In addition to ballet, I have a considerable background in butoh. I've played a lot of ghosts.

I primarily dance in other people's work, but I've done some of my own choreography as well, usually in collaboration. I've choreographed for collaborations with a visual artist who does wearable sculpture and with a playwright.

How would you describe your current dance practice?

I take class 365 days a year. I'm one of the only people I know at this point in their career who literally takes class every day. I take mostly ballet class, though I also do a lot of jazz and some contemporary. Most days of the week, I'm also rehearsing in one project or another. I generally have three or four projects going on at any given time. In addition, I am a strong believer in conditioning. I lift weight most days. I also teach athletics to disabled youth; I have a certification as an integrative conditioning coach through the American College of Sports Medicine.

When you tell people you are a dancer, what are the most common reactions you receive?

Though I use a white cane, a lot of people don't know what a white cane is for. They don't know that it means I'm blind. I generally have to explain. People who know I'm blind often think that dance is some kind of hobby or cute inspirational thing. No dude, I'm cutthroat; this is my career.

A lot of people assume things about the dancing I must do. They wonder how I know where I am. I am patient and happy to explain the minutia to people if they are asking me those questions in good faith. I'm more patient than most, but it is kind of sad. Most people don't even know a blind person. They don't understand what it means to be blind.

What are some ways people discuss dance with regards to disability that you feel carry problematic implications or assumptions?

There are two categories of feedback I find problematic. One is: "I couldn't even tell you are blind/visually impaired," as if I'm trying

to hide it or I'm ashamed of the fact. Why would I be embarrassed? This is who I am, and this is the body I work with. I think they are trying to assure me that they couldn't tell I have a disability. The other feedback generally comes from people who know ahead of time that they are going to see a blind performer. I think it colors their perception of what they are about to see so strongly that they are not able to see the content of what I've done, and instead are fixated on seeing some blind lady dance. It's almost as if my identity is too distracting that they can't pay attention to the performance itself.

Do you believe there are adequate training opportunities for dancers with disabilities? If not, what areas would you specifically like to see improved?

I'm only going to speak for blind and visually impaired dancers, but I feel like the educational opportunities available take the worst possible approach. They treat the blind or visually impaired dancer's body like a marionette and don't encourage bodily autonomy. In other words, the teacher moves the student around, which basically prevents the student from learning how to dance.

Nobody should ever touch a blind person without saying something first. I don't know why this is so hard for people to understand. I know a lot of blind people are accustomed to being manhandled, but it's not the mindset I want serious dance students to cultivate about themselves.

There are certain skills I believe a visually impaired or blind person needs to have prior to studying dance seriously, which are directional hearing, internal balance, and foot sensitivity. I created a workshop called Dark Room Ballet which develops these skills. However, I haven't gotten to teach it to many blind people, though I keep trying. I've mostly been teaching it to sighted people, which is kind of sad. But if a blind or visually impaired person can cultivate those skills first, they can study any dance technique they want.

I really like when teachers use verbal descriptions. That's one of the reasons why I'm still in ballet class; I know my terms, so I can listen and comprehend. I feel that the more contemporary tradition of just having dancers follow the teacher or choreographer is very inaccessible. Being able to describe the steps or choreography is vital for visually impaired dancers.

I also like when dance teachers offer their own body for blind students to touch and learn from for more complex shapes and patterns. It's much more respectful than moving the dancer like a piece of clay.

> "People who know I'm blind often think that dance is some kind of hobby or cute inspirational thing. No dude, I'm cutthroat; this is my career.

Would you like to see disability in dance assimilated into the mainstream?

Something I like about our disability arts community is that in a way we're pioneers. We don't have to replicate the crappy things about dance culture that already exist. We don't have to encourage dancers to trash themselves physically and ignore their wellbeing. We don't have to replicate tyrannical choreographers. We have a cleaner slate. I would actually like if non-disabled dance culture would assimilate to us.

With regards to open classes, I sneak into open class every day. My money is the same as anyone else's. Sometimes I ask the teacher for permission; usually I don't. If you feel confident enough that you can be in the room and no harm can come to you, do as you want. If somebody treats you wrong, they're breaking the law.

As for performance venues and festivals, why would they not consider disabled performers and artists for any program? We're spectacular. We're talented. We're creative. We're coming up with some of the newest and most innovative ideas.

Once I auditioned for a dance company and had a great audition, but the choreographer told me that, while he liked the way I moved, he wasn't sure if he wanted his company to go in *that* direction, as if disability is a distraction from his genius. I don't know what to do about people like that. I don't want to collaborate with people who aren't thrilled to collaborate with me.

On the other hand, I sometimes get approached for projects or companies I'm definitely uncomfortable with. I was recently approached by a playwright wanting to make an inspirational semi-autobiographical play about me but with a tragic romance. That's called fetishism.

What is your preferred term for the field?

I like the term "visually impaired" because it's like a big tent and it doesn't ask people to go into the minutia of how much sight they have and thus create a sight hierarchy, which I think is counterproductive. I like "disability arts" because we all have multiple artistic skills, whether it's dance, music, acting, writing, or visual arts. As for me personally, I call myself "blind lady" or "blind lady dancer."

In your perspective, is the field improving with time?

I feel like it is improving in certain ways. Alice Sheppard won a Bessie award, and that was one of the greatest things that ever happened. I want to be Alice when I grow up. However, while the disability arts community is becoming bigger and more exciting within it, getting non-disabled people to support us is still challenging.

For example, in order for me to be safe in my performance space, I need a little time in the space before tech rehearsals. That's just basic. If I can't learn the dimensions and feel the floor texture, I can't perform safely. Sometimes venues don't understand that. On the phone or over email, they'll tell me I can't come in early, but when I appear and I have my cane and am wearing shades, they say, "Oh my god, what can I do for you? Can I guide you around by the arm?" It's this weird bipolar relationship. On the phone they deny me access, but when they meet me in person, they suddenly feel guilty. It's very complicated and stressful and puts me in a lot of uncomfortable situations. I was able to get an hour and a half on my stage when I performed last month. I had to work really hard really fast. If I was not as skilled as I am, I wouldn't be able to pull it off. This scenario happens to me repeatedly.

Any other thoughts?

What I would really love is to just do my work. That's all I care about. It's been so difficult for me to acquire the skills I have so that I can work at the level I do. I wouldn't do this if it wasn't the most important thing in the universe to me. I'd sacrifice just about anything else. I breathe dance every minute of my life. And I'm a hustler. I take every gig I can get unless I think it is inspiration porn. I'm in class every day. I'm constantly building my skills and talking to people about the art I do. I'm always striving. I work so hard, but some people think I just show up onstage and manifest as a fascinating other-worldly alien creature. No man, I'm a straight up jock hustler. I have a gig every month, and it's going to be like that until the day I die.

HAI COHEN

Hai Cohen *was born in Jerusalem and became paralyzed from the chest down after jumping into the shallow water of a swimming pool. He became a music editor in the army radio station and studied Philosophy. Hai graduated from the Sam Spiegel Film and Television School and went on to create documentary films. He is a dancer, teacher, and co-manager with Tali Wertheim at Vertigo Power of Balance, which operates out of Vertigo Eco Art Village near Jerusalem. He has practiced contact improvisation since 2000 and leads workshops and projects in disabled and non-disabled contact improvisation in Israel and abroad.*

"I Would Like to See Good Dance, Period"

This interview was conducted by Silva Laukkanen in April 2020

How did you get into dance and what have been some highlights in your dance history?

I was injured when I was 13. I jumped into shallow water in a swimming pool. I got back to so-called "normal life" in high school. In Israel we have the army so, after high school, I volunteered for the army and became a music editor at the army radio station. After that, I studied film for five years and ended up making documentaries as well as experimenting with video. While doing some research for a film in 2000, I met a dancer who invited me to an integrated dance workshop. I said no, that it was not my interest, but she insisted so eventually I joined. The workshop was through Vertigo Dance Company and hosted by Adam Benjamin for the creation of a new piece. The workshop was three days long and was very powerful for me.

After the workshop, Adam went back to England and then came back to Israel to start working on the piece. It was two or three months of rehearsal and, a year after the workshop in 2001, we premiered the piece. There were four participants with disabilities who joined the original cast. The name of the piece was *Power of Balance*. We performed it for three years.

At the same time, I was researching contact improvisation with Tali Wertheim. We wanted to figure out how to continue integrated dance in Israel. One year into performing *Power of Balance*, I began teaching. It was the start of a branch of Vertigo Dance Company, also called Power of Balance, that is an integrated dance center for people with and without disabilities.

Tali and I taught workshops and created some works for the stage, including a duet and a trio with another dancer, Maya Resheff, who is not disabled. The trio, *11,711 Stone Steps at Nikko*, was a highlight for me because it incorporated haiku. I try to incorporate haiku into everything I touch. When I worked in film, I tried to create cinematic haikus, and with this piece I was trying to make a dance haiku within the structure and spirit by using contact improvisation.

I've also been part of the Israeli contact improv association that has been around for many years. I think the first festival was around the time I started dancing, and it grew slowly over eight or nine years. It is very significant for our work, which is not only directed to the integrated dance field but also to the contact improvisation field in Israel and around the world.

As far as other highlights, in 2007, Alex Shmurak (a dancer and a friend) and I did a collaboration with a company in Ethiopia where we choreographed *Adugna*. I also made a documentary about the project. In 2013, we did a co-production with Gerda König called *HOMEZONE*. Now, we're in the middle of a new process by choreographer Sharon Fridman, who is originally from Israel but lives in Madrid. It's his first time working with an integrated cast, but he's a rising star in the dance world. I'm not actually dancing in this piece, but I'm helping to manage it, so I'm very much involved. The piece has 10 dancers, five with disabilities and five without.

How would you describe your current dance practice?

I teach with Tali a training for integrated contact improvisation. The course is a full day once a week, and it's a two-year program. Of course, it's integrated for participants of all kinds of abilities. We're trying to make the model co-teaching in an integrated team, one teacher with a disability and one without. That has a lot of power. This is our main practice for the past four years. We also do one-time projects and classes, like with a dance department in a high school together with the special education kids, or offering professional development for teachers in integrated dance so they have the tools to work with any kid.

When you tell people you are a dancer, what are the most common reactions you receive?

Many people think I'm joking, and then they see I'm not smiling. Usually I don't have the energy to explain. Most people just have a question mark. Some ask, "With your wheelchair?"

When I teach, there are people in the class who at first don't know I'm the teacher. I sense that they think I'm something exceptional but they still see dancing with me as an option. Maybe because the contact improvisation world is more open, dancing with someone with a disability is more of an option.

> "I would like to see good dance, period. I don't want integrated dance to be promoted just because it's integrated dance. It should be good. There's still **not enough good dance.**

What are some ways people discuss dance with regards to disability that you feel carry problematic implications or assumptions?

When I go into a restaurant and there are stairs, I don't get mad. I ask someone to help me up the stairs. I don't have the energy to get angry. Of course I believe that integrated dance should be much more supported, and I hope that in the future we can teach anyone who wants to dance. I feel like I have two worlds; I really believe in this when I teach and present work, but when it's personal, I find I'm not as involved. It's more enjoyable not to be angry so much.

I'm not so interested in what people think about the choreographed work. There are so many opinions in the world. Some I believe; many I don't believe. I've learned how to look at the creation process from my own point of view, from what I wish to see in dance or in film. For some, my films are slow and boring, but it's something I like to see, like an endless shot where nothing happens. I like to see time as the value of discovery.

Maybe it's different when I think about participants in my classes. There's a variety of experiences within the same class. Some enjoy it, some not. I am giving a class though, which is different than giving a performance. I don't give a performance for the audience. It's more about creating beauty in the world. It doesn't need to have relevance to others. But when I'm teaching, it matters to me what the students' experience is. If I see someone suffering or having a hard time, I feel responsibility. But at the same time, I can accept that people don't always enjoy my teaching. It's fine.

As for the press, this new piece we're working on has got me thinking a bit different than I was before. Before, I would have said to try and see it as professional dance. Now I think it's more about the approach of the integration. In this new piece, Sharon is a bit brave. He is putting disability onstage and showing it as something weak and at the same time showing its power. He has managed to show these two qualities that actually everyone has. People with disabilities sometimes need more help. This is a reality and not something we need to hide or wrap in beauty.

For example, one of the dancers has cerebral palsy and walks with crutches. He can also walk without them but his balance is not good and he has a funny walk with short steps. In the piece, he walks without the crutches. It's very powerful to see the weakness and difference, to see the naked walk without the crutches. The crutches hide the original walk. They not only help him physically, they also help to normalize him. But if he walks the way he does, without crutches, I can see it, feel it, and benefit from it. Appreciating this kind of detail is something different than what I thought before.

The press should understand that disability in dance isn't something to portray as something that it's not. Still, see it as a professional act. And of course, it should not be portrayed as charity or therapy.

Do you believe there are adequate training opportunities for dancers with disabilities? If not, what areas would you specifically like to see improved?

Of course not. Every studio, after school program, and university program should have the ability to accept anyone with any disability. But of course, there is a lot of work to be done. What happens sometimes is people open their doors to disabled students without the ability to teach them. You need the knowledge to understand how to work with a diversity of bodies and abilities before you open the doors. Many difficulties and frustrations can arise.

We need teacher trainings to start with. And then I would prioritize the schools. It should start from the beginning, even for students without disabilities to be open to this from a young age and see students with disabilities as participants.

Would you like to see disability in dance assimilated into the mainstream?

Yes, of course. It should be treated the same as other dance fields. It should be expected to be as good and as professional and be given the same space and recognition. Saying that, I'm not sure how I feel about integrated dance festivals. They can offer options that other festivals can't. But at the same time, it can feel like a ghetto with an inner dialogue only within the community.

I would like to see good dance, period. If it's integrated dance, then maybe I would be happier because I'm closer to it. But I would just love to see a good performance. I don't want integrated dance to be promoted just because it's integrated dance. It should be good. There's still not enough good dance.

What is your preferred term for the field?

I'm really tired of dealing with terms. In Hebrew, it's even worse; it's much easier in English. In Hebrew, the word "disabled" is like an insult. I used to not answer when people used that word. Over the years I've gotten tired and now I use it myself and I don't mind. Still, I agree there's a lot of meaning behind the words we choose. At Power of Balance, we're using "integrated," but "inclusive" is also great. "People with diverse bodies" is also strong.

In your perspective, is the field improving with time?

Of course, yes. I think there are big steps. I can see development from our center in Israel and more support from the government. There's still a long way to go, but it's really different from what it was. There are more audiences and disabled participants who want to experience this.

Kris Lenzo

Kris Lenzo *transitioned to dance after more than two decades as a wheelchair athlete; he was a national champion in both wheelchair basketball and wheelchair track multiple times. Since 2003, he has danced with MOMENTA in Chicago, Illinois. He has performed at Spring to Dance in St. Louis several times and has also appeared in Dance Chicago, Duets for my Valentine, Bodies of Work's Disability, Art, and Culture Festival, Counter Balance (I-VII), and at Chicago's Disability Pride Parade. Kris is also a teacher in MOMENTA's EveryBody Can Dance! workshops and was a 2015 3Arts awardee.*

"An Opportunity to Educate"

This interview was conducted by Silva Laukkanen in April and August 2020

How did you get into dance and what have been some highlights in your dance history?

My youngest daughter, Olivia, went to preschool at the Academy of Movement and Music, a local dance and music school. I asked the owner, Stephanie Clemens, to install a ramp to the building so I could pick up my daughter. Stephanie was also the co-founder of MOMENTA Dance Company. To Stephanie's credit, she raised money to put in a ramp, as well as made the bathrooms wheelchair accessible and put in an elevator. At that point, Stephanie wanted to commemorate making the building accessible by creating a dance for MOMENTA featuring dancers with and without disabilities, and asked if I would like to be in it. My initial reaction was, "No, not in the least," but then she said if any of my daughters wanted to be in it with me, they could. Olivia (who was four or five years old at the time) said she wanted to be a part. Stephanie also asked me if I knew any other dancers in wheelchairs. I had seen Ginger Lane perform in a production somewhere, so I recommended her. And then there were two twin sisters who would be a part. One had cerebral palsy and the other didn't have a disability. The five of us did a piece choreographed by Larry Ipple. This was in 2003.

Dancing was a lot more fun and interesting than I thought it would be. The piece had an original composer and live music. This was my first time performing, and I just thought that was how it always was. It was a nice way to start dancing. Playing basketball, I often was out of town at games, whereas the dance rehearsals were half a mile from my home, and I got to spend more time with my daughter.

As far as pieces that I've done that are highlights, one of them would be *Ashes* in 2004, the year after I started dancing. In the piece, I hung upside down for 10 minutes and lifted this dancer repeatedly. It was challenging to figure out how to support me upside down and we tried various options. The piece ended up being really unique. The audience could only see half my body, and they couldn't see the apparatus supporting me, so it was like I was hanging from the clouds. We did the piece until 2013, and performing it was always a highlight.

MOMENTA has performed maybe six times at Spring to Dance in St. Louis. Every time we've gone, it's always had integrated work. It's a well-run festival with two theaters showing two concerts a night. High caliber companies are presented, and the tickets are affordable. That was always a highlight to be a part of. Another highlight was being a part of Bodies of Work's Disability, Art, and Culture Festival, organized by Carrie Sandahl, in 2006 and 2013.

But the biggest highlight of my career was receiving the 3Arts Residency Fellowship in 2015. It was $25,000 and really validating artistically.

How would you describe your current dance practice?

The amount of time my dance practice takes can vary quite a bit. It's not a full-time job, but it disproportionately feeds my soul. Dance connects me to art. I don't usually take classes, but I teach in MOMENTA's EveryBody Can Dance! workshops. There are six or seven of those each year. When there's an upcoming production, I am in rehearsal more, and then my schedule is less intense afterward. I go to contact improv on Sundays sometimes, and I exercise on my own in order to have a smaller list of what I can't do anymore. I was 43 when I started dancing and I'm 60 now.

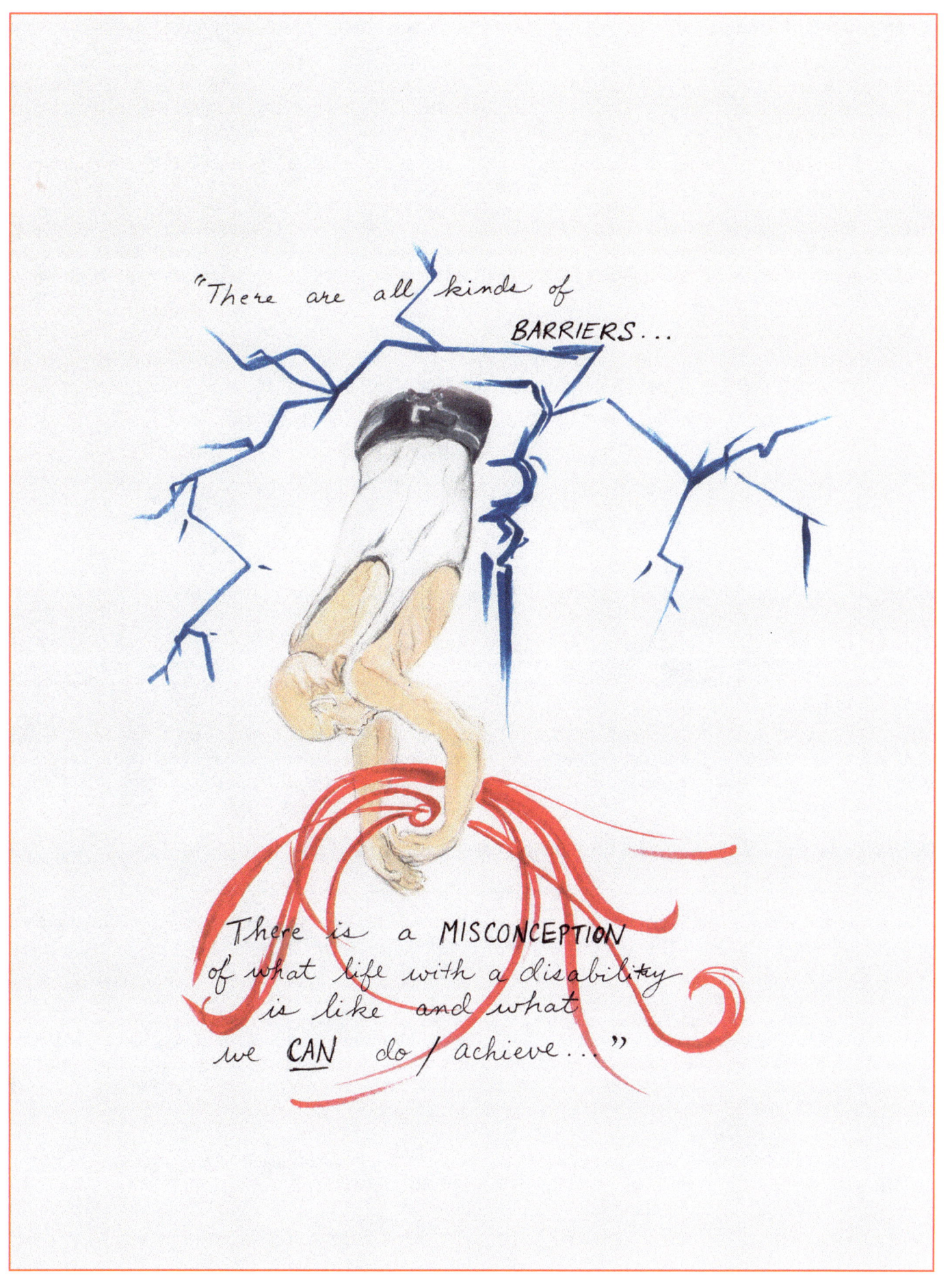

When you tell people you are a dancer, what are the most common reactions you receive?

"What?" Sometimes people think I'm joking. They might ask, "How does that work?" I'd say confusion and curiosity are the most common responses. Now that I've been dancing with MOMENTA for so long and I know so many of the families who have come through the school, people often tell me they saw me in a show. Still, a much higher percentage of the population knows what wheelchair basketball is versus what disability or integrated dance is. I look at it as an opportunity to educate someone.

There are all kinds of barriers that people with disabilities run into – architectural, medical, economic – and two of the barriers are a misconception of what life with a disability is like and what we can do/achieve, as well as a social awkwardness. A goal of mine is to reduce those barriers and create more connection between people with and without disabilities. I want to create more awareness as well as increase comfort-level; so many people without disabilities are uncomfortable around people with disabilities. I would like to see a world in which everyone knows five people with a disability. Then we start to look at people with disabilities and just be curious and relaxed. Performances can play an important role. Someone might think, "I've never seen a person with a disability dance before; what else can they do?"

> "A much higher percentage of the population knows what wheelchair basketball is versus what disability or integrated dance is. I look at it as an opportunity to educate someone.

What are some ways people discuss dance with regards to disability that you feel carry problematic implications or assumptions?

One response I hear a lot that rubs me the wrong way is when people see me perform and say, "I didn't even see the wheelchair." I'm like, "You should have!" In some ways, it can be viewed as a compliment, but it's a backhanded one. I consider my wheelchair an extension of my body, both when I played basketball and when I dance.

I did sports for about 20 years playing basketball, road racing, and track, and road racing got the most coverage. At the time, wheelchair racing was somewhat new. There was a fair amount of inspiration-porn back then. But for dance, I can't recall that narrative being applied to me. Maybe that's because Chicago has such a vibrant disability arts scene in general. I'm the fourth disabled artist to get the 3Arts award, which is specifically geared toward people of color, women, and people with disabilities.

Do you believe there are adequate training opportunities for dancers with disabilities?

Probably not. It depends on where you are. Here in Chicago, we've got a strong disabled dance community.

However, I remember a woman who was a double amputee came to one of our EveryBody Can Dance! workshops and wanted to come again the following week, but we hold them only once a month and, even then, only six or seven months out of the year. It's hard to build momentum only once a month. Even in places like ours that have a robust disability dance community, the training is limited.

The number of dancers is also limited. This speaks to the problem of identifying, grooming, and developing new dancers. There's an inherent problem in that, as far as people who acquire disabilities from an accident, they're much more likely to be male because we can be a bit reckless, relatively speaking. And most guys are not interested in performative dance. I choreographed a piece 12 or 15 years ago, and I had the kids tell me a little about their backgrounds before we got started. This boy Tommy said he's been dancing since he was nine or 10, and there are usually barely any other guys besides him. He said it used to bother him that his dance classes had two guys and 16 women, but it doesn't anymore.

Beyond teaching in MOMENTA'S EveryBody Can Dance! workshops, I'd personally like to get involved in teaching dance at local rehab hospitals. With dance, people become less self-conscious and start moving freely. The spirit of it gives people more stamina than they think they have. They improve their wheelchair mobility and expressiveness too.

Would you like to see disability in dance assimilated into the mainstream?

Definitely. Most of the performances I've been in have been integrated settings where there are dancers with and without disabilities, but I've also been part of concerts where every piece was disability dance. Whatever works. When I used to play wheelchair basketball, I enjoyed watching other teams play. I thought it was interesting enough to watch that it could have been more popular than it was. But how do you bring people to it? Any way you can introduce people to this work makes sense. Reaching one person is valuable. I don't worry much about how extensive the audience is. It's out of my control.

It's great if we have dancers with disabilities performing professionally. But just like with sports where most of the kids playing won't go professional, it's great just to get kids and adults with disabilities involved in dance, especially in inclusive dance settings, just so they learn that everyone can dance and realize the many benefits of dance.

What is your preferred term for the field?

For me personally, I like "dancer" or "disabled dancer." As far as the name of the field, I kind of like "inclusive dance." It sounds inviting.

When I first became disabled, the idea of being "temporarily able-bodied" didn't resonate at all with me; either you were disabled or not. Since then, my dad got Parkinson's before he died, then my brother Peter had a head injury that resulted in epilepsy. A friend of mine who was really into fitness and health had a skiing accident and is now a quadriplegic. At that point, I understood and appreciated the term. The aging process is disabling too.

In your perspective, is the field improving with time?

I'd say overall it's getting more well-known because there's been more coverage of dancers with disabilities, like when AXIS was on *So You Think You Can Dance*. People either know about the field or they don't. I still run into some who haven't heard of disability dance.

Any other thoughts?

I remember once talking about dance with another disabled athlete who said he liked watching dancers because he could see them stretching their envelope of movement vocabulary. Twenty years later when I started to dance, I remembered and appreciated that comment.

CHRISTELLE DREYER

Christelle Dreyer is a dancer and graphic designer from Cape Town, South Africa, who participates in dance styles varying from contemporary to ballroom and Latin dance. Through Remix Dance Project, a physically integrated dance company in Cape Town, Christelle has taught dance to schoolchildren. In 2014, she performed as part of the UNI Global Union Women's Conference. In 2017, she received the Cultural Affairs Award from the Western Cape Government for Contribution by Person with Disability to The Arts.

"We Have to Prove We Can Move"

This interview was conducted by Silva Laukkanen in May 2019

How did you get into dance and what have been some highlights in your dance history?

I got into dance while I was in high school. Dance companies would come to my school and introduce the students to different styles. At first I felt forced to do it. Back then, we were supposed to choose something to do, whether it was chess or sports or an art, but I'm still dancing all these years later.

A highlight was teaching schoolchildren as part of Remix Dance Project with Nicola Elliott and Malcolm Black. We did a collaboration with kids in the normal schools and kids in the disabled schools. We met with them once a week. At first the kids were so scared of each other. The kids from the normal school were afraid to touch the disabled kids. Same on the other side; they really didn't interact and just stuck to their own groups. What we would do is put them in a circle, one disabled kid and one normal kid side by side. Spacing them like that, it forced them to interact. Then we started going around doing introductions and games. By the last two sessions, we couldn't even get them to focus because they were friends. They wanted to have sleepovers. We did this process at three or four schools at a time. Monday we would be at one school, then Tuesday at the next school. At the end of the term we had a show where each school would perform. Then me and an able-bodied person would do a duet to show the kids some moves. They got to experience performing on a real stage with lights and proper sound, and parents and teachers could come watch. We tried to do as many schools as possible. It was so successful and so cool to see.

About five years ago, I attended AXIS Dance Company's summer intensive. I learned that my dance technique as a disabled person isn't too bad. I was expecting to be the worst person in the room from not having the guidance I need.

In South Africa, 90 percent of the time I am the only person with a wheelchair in dance classes. If it is an advanced contemporary class, people are leaping and going fast. I have to keep up or get out of the way. If I don't, the other dancers get irritated. I am forced to pick up the combinations without pause and translate choreography that isn't meant for a wheelchair user. There is no time for me to say, "Wait, I have to figure out my wheels, the counts, and the spacing." Everything is at the same time, and there isn't someone to teach me how to translate movement because a lot of the time the teacher isn't trained to teach disabled people. I'm in the class but not really in the class because they don't know what to do with me.

In 2019, I was part of the Disability Inclusion Lab at UCLA. I learned so much. In South Africa, I haven't had that much exposure to disability dance. Like ballet or hip-hop, it is a genre. We looked at what it would be defined as or what it would look like; how you would use wheelchairs or crutches to move around the space, for example.

We also looked at the concept of disability culture. It was interesting to hear different people's views. The other participants were fascinated that I was from South Africa. To them, it is this magical land with lions. But I live in a normal city. However, the advancement of disability culture is not the same back home. They couldn't understand that there are certain things they expect and take for granted. The idea of basic accessibility in a building or in society is not happening in South Africa. They would say to me, "Oh, but you are so complacent." I am not complacent. They are living with actual rights. The things they have access to in their everyday communities are luxuries I don't have at home. I am not complacent; there was just so much more access than I was used to.

How would you describe your current dance practice?

Currently, I'm not with a company or any organization. I'm solo. I take any dance classes I can find – contemporary, contact improv, basically anything that can keep me fit until I find my next project. However, there are no classes that might help me as a disabled dancer use my wheelchair better. I figure it out for myself. If the choreography includes counts, I have to combine two counts into one, because I have to push my chair at the same time as doing the movement. So I'm using both the teacher's counts and my own counts. It's very difficult.

In general, I try to always keep myself immersed in movement. I'm freelancing, but I also started school recently. I'm doing my master's in graphic design, so my time is split. I stopped dancing for a while because, to be honest, dancing doesn't really pay the bills. But it wasn't working; I had to start dancing again. I don't think I'll stop dancing unless my body tells me it doesn't want to dance. I don't know what form that will always take though.

> " There are only a **handful of us dancers** with disabilities here in South Africa, so we must fight our way into what is known as the mainstream. We have to **prove we actually can move.** People don't see disabled dancers as real dancers who are credible.

When you tell people you are a dancer, what are the most common reactions you receive?

Some people are confused, like, "What do you mean?" Other people say, "Oh, that's nice. It must keep you busy," like dance is a hobby that keeps me occupied because I'm disabled. People also wonder how I dance.

What are some ways people discuss dance with regards to disability that you feel carry problematic implications or assumptions?

There are only a handful of us dancers with disabilities here in South Africa, so we must fight our way into what is known as the mainstream. We have to prove we actually can move. People don't see disabled dancers as real dancers who are credible. So when the press describes us, they don't take us as seriously as – I don't know what to call it…normal? other? – dancers. Even in the descriptions of our shows, you can tell they don't consider us at the same level. A review might say, "The disabled dancers are integrated with the other dancers." That language puts us in a box. Can't you just say, "the dancers" and leave out "integrated" or "disabled" in front of the word "dance"? Can't we just be a dance company?

Reviewers always make what I do a bigger deal than it needs to be. They'll make a big deal about if I lift my leg, writing, "And she pointed her toes." But all the other dancers onstage were pointing their toes as well. I'm not a novelty act. I want people to see me on par with the other dancers. Obviously, if I am a better dancer then say that. But don't say it's amazing that I can lift my arm because I'm disabled.

I also have problems with auditions. The announcement will say it's an open audition but when I show up, they look at me like, "Why are you here?" It's not really an open audition. I've noticed though that audition announcements are starting to get more specific, like with height requirements. It makes it harder for me to find auditions.

Disabled people are equal to anyone else. We're not separate. The quality of our work should not be based on the disability but on our actual skills as dancers. I want for people to see me as a dancer, and that I have the necessary ability and skill to be a dancer. I want to be seen as a professional in the field, not someone who is trying to be a dancer.

Do you believe there are adequate training opportunities for dancers with disabilities? If not, what areas would you specifically like to see improved?

I think teachers really do try to learn and adapt for their disabled students. Not all my experiences are negative. If my initial experiences in the classroom were negative, I wouldn't still be dancing. I think I've been lucky in that way, that I've had some teachers who could actually teach me.

Would you like to see disability in dance assimilated into the mainstream?

Most definitely. People in Cape Town say they want disability rights, accessibility, inclusion, integration, all those fancy words. They can make laws about it and hold meetings and workshops, but I think when we actually do it, that's when it happens. You have to actually go to the schools and encourage the kids to integrate. And disabled people need to be onstage for other people to see. Shows shouldn't necessarily be about being disabled, just include disabled people in performances, on TV, or in movies.

As far as dance, I want to see disability dance as its own genre, but I also want to see it integrated. When I am forced to be in the same space as everybody else, it gives my technique strength. Sometimes that is exactly what is needed to grow as a dancer, to be forced to push our limits, to be forced to keep up with the other dancers.

That being said, I always find it so entertaining when I'm in a dance class and the teacher says to stand up straight. I just start laughing because my spine can't be straight. I can be "up," but my spine isn't straight.

What is your preferred term for the field?

I think they normally say integrated, but since there are so few of us dancing with disabilities in South Africa, we all just say what we feel. Terms or words have never been that important to me. Whether people call me disabled or crippled, or call it integrated dance or inclusive dance, I don't mind. Words don't diminish me in any way. However, I know there are other people who get offended by certain terminologies. As important as inclusion is, it's not as important to choose a word as it is to get on with the process.

It should just be called "dancing." Especially with academic people, they often try to overanalyze things. I don't understand why it needs to be labeled as "disabled" or "non-disabled."

In your perspective, is the field improving with time?

In South Africa, it is happening so small you almost can't see it, but it is happening. People like me are making it happen. I impose myself, whether other dancers want me in the space or not. I sometimes go to a studio and I can see they don't really want me there, but at least they are polite. Three weeks later, they get used to me and then they start to like me.

MAIJA KARHUNEN

Maija Karhunen *works with choreographers and directors in Finland and Europe. She studied dance and choreography in Finland, the Netherlands, and Germany. Her interests lie in the all-encompassing performativity of the human, questions of power, intimacy, the personal, and the grotesque. She works also in the field of dance writing and critique.*

"I Can Make Space For Myself"
This interview was conducted by Silva Laukkanen in August 2018

How did you get into dance and what have been some highlights in your dance history?

I was attracted to dancing because it was my sister's hobby, and I wanted to do the same. I was in my early teenage years and it was quite difficult to find a place where, as a disabled teenager, I could dance as a hobby. My physiotherapist was working in a school for disabled children and there she found an announcement about a group. When I got older, I did some workshops with Alito Alessi and started to dance with people who were doing integrated dance in Finland at that time. I was thinking about a completely different career, however, and that was to work as a journalist. With a friend's encouragement, I did one year of training in dance and somatics. I moved more than I had done before, and my body changed a lot. Then I studied for short periods in some dance and choreography schools in England, Holland, and Germany. A big turning point was to go to all these dance schools which hadn't usually had disabled students before. At that point and earlier also, I was very active; I was just so eager to dance and learn wherever I could, so I just showed up and didn't question if I could be there or not. For some reason, I had the courage and confidence to do that…it's a mystery to myself how I did that. A highlight is also when I found myself working in the field professionally. I have already worked with so many interesting people. That's definitely a constant highlight.

How would you describe your current dance practice?

I work with very different choreographers, so my dance practice varies a lot accordingly. In both pieces that I'm working on at the moment, music is a lot of the focus. One of the works is on electronic music, so it's a lot of dancing to beats. The other work has classical music in it, but interestingly, the questions are quite similar: What is it to dance to music and be as close to music as possible? In both works, we are also asking: What is togetherness on stage and what does it mean to dance together? As a collective, what does it do to individuality?

When you tell people you are a dancer, what are the most common reactions you receive?

In Finland, dance is a very popular hobby but, as an art form, it's not very familiar to many people. The question often is, "Do you dance alone or with a partner, and to what kind of music?" People's association is often social dance, dancing to music, not the art form or something that somebody would do professionally. People associate it also with competitive wheelchair dancing.

In the professional dance field, there is a lot of positive interest. People think it's great that I'm a dancer, and there are also political reasons for that, which I embrace but which can sometimes feel like a big responsibility and one-dimensional. Still, I try to be a bit more vocal about myself, saying, "Hey, I'm here and I'm also dancing," because I realize the political importance of that. But when an individual carries that message, it's often a bit difficult. For example, I get the most positive feedback when I talk about my experience exactly from the point of view of a disabled person, which feels strange to me. It's a lot about people's projections on me. I find there can be a lot of expectations that I, as a disabled person, must have very special genius thoughts or my experience must be so very different from other people's. It can be this othering. A fellow artist just said in a rehearsal situation that they are nervous to dance with me. It's human, I guess, because many artists never seem to have encountered a disabled person. If they then say they are very aware of the world that surrounds them, or say that they pay attention to diversity or whatever, I find it a bit hypocritical.

What are some ways people discuss dance with regards to disability that you feel carry problematic implications or assumptions?

Exactly this, what I already mentioned, all these different projections, special attention, or othering. People might want to see me empowered because that gives them a good conscience or whatever. Or they want to make space for me. I can make space for myself when I need and want to! Many times, I find myself wondering what people actually are thinking. People are very polite, and I get scared they might think I'm too fragile to receive honest feedback (which I am of course!) and they feel they have to like everything I do. And of course when I get grants and opportunities, I think it's only because I'm there to fill a diversity quota, like I'm the disabled one they must support. So I struggle a lot to believe in myself because of all this.

Maybe we also in some situations need to put a disabled person on a pedestal and just see a disabled person as strong, amazing, and great. But we've seen too much of these kinds of individual stories and it has risks, obviously. I think it would be good that we all became more aware of our projections on others. What we don't talk about that much is the structural position of disabled people in society. Maybe that brave and courageous person had wealthy, educated, white parents and therefore had a lot of support, and it was actually quite easy to become courageous and brave. Disabled people are not equal in relation to non-disabled people but also not among themselves. Depending on society and what kind of support, resources, and accessibility is available, just doing something like choosing dance as a profession is not necessarily an act of bravery. Also, reporters could be asked to reflect on how often and in what roles a disabled person is represented in their media. Are there disabled people represented as experts of different fields, not just through their disability? Are there disabled reporters working in the media?

Do you believe there are adequate training opportunities for dancers with disabilities? If not, what areas would you specifically like to see improved?

Definitely not. In Finland, for example, professional dance training still has a very conventional attitude; it's a given that it cannot include people with disabilities. Educational institutions change slowly, although I think many of them would like to be more open and could be practically, but maybe it's bureaucracy that stops them. There's a lot of inclusive training opportunities in improvisation, but in what could be called dance techniques, there aren't so many opportunities. I guess a variety is lacking. But I've also learned a lot through just working. You can find input from so many different experiences, it doesn't just have to be established training and dance education.

> "People might want to see me empowered because that gives them a good conscience or whatever. Or they want to make space for me. I can make space for myself when I need and want to!

Would you like to see disability in dance assimilated into the mainstream?

I guess it's a question for everyone to figure out themselves, about mainstream and marginal and what one's goal and personal interest is. I'm not interested in staying in a category separated from possibilities or connections with many kinds of people, but I'm not interested in creating new normativity either. It's quite hard to imagine answers to this question. I would like to get rid of othering because I yearn for connection. I think disability can bring an awareness that could be beneficial for other people as well. For example, I sometimes need practical help from others in working situations. Maybe the presence of a disabled person can highlight that we are dependent on each other, and it could be more acceptable to ask for help, as an opposition to the individualistic culture that we live in now.

What is your preferred term for the field?

I guess "integration" is always referring to someone outside the norm or mainstream being integrated into it. "Inclusion" carries different meanings; it's about including someone as they are and who they are, not expecting them to change themselves.

In your perspective, is the field improving with time?

I want to question why we need this category or field in the first place. I personally don't believe in creating this separate field where people with disabilities can do dance and art but not elsewhere. That's also not how I live my life. But I do understand that there are people for whom the work is very important, and it provides a chance to do something when so many opportunities and possibilities are generally not available. I think it's also a lot about identity: How much is disability part of identity? How much does mixed abilities dance want to stay in the margin and be a kind of subculture in the dance field? That's also okay. But often within the field, there is the desire to stop categorizing. If that's the desire, then one needs to take the step and not create this category.

It's difficult to say if the field is improving with time because I don't follow it so thoroughly, but I think there are some interesting people who work in this field and I've also seen interesting works. I think it's good the field questions itself maybe a bit more, for example exactly which term to use and so on.

ANTOINE HUNTER

Antoine Hunter *is an African American Deaf producer, choreographer, dancer, actor, and advocate. He has performed throughout the Bay Area and internationally, and is the founder and director of Urban Jazz Dance. In 2013, he initiated the Bay Area International Deaf Dance Festival, the first of its kind. He teaches dance and ASL in both hearing and Deaf communities, and is on faculty at East Bay Center for the Performing Arts, Shawl-Anderson Dance Center, Youth in Arts, and Dance-A-Vision.*

"I Move My Body and I Communicate"
This interview was conducted by Silva Laukkanen in July 2018

How did you get into dance and what have been some highlights in your dance history?

Dance has always been part of me. From the day I was born, I have always been moving. Growing up in the Bay Area, especially in Oakland, breakdancing was very popular. But my love of dance started by watching Oakland Ballet Company's *Nutcracker*. Being Deaf, when I would watch TV or go to the movies, I couldn't connect with what I was seeing, even though I was watching the same event as everyone around me. I would miss all the jokes. When I saw Oakland Ballet, it was wonderful. No one was talking onstage; instead, everyone was dancing to communicate. It showed me that I can use art and dance to communicate with the world.

However, my mom couldn't afford to take me to dance lessons, so I had to wait until high school. My high school dance teacher taught modern and jazz and had a lot of energy and fire. Whenever she danced, it was always with passion. She made me want to dance like that too. She didn't treat me differently even though I was the only Deaf student in her class. She didn't make me feel like an outcast.

I was so hooked on dance that I wasn't really thinking about college. My senior year, my dance teacher asked me what my plans were, and I said I had no idea. She urged me to audition for the California Institute of the Arts. That audition class was the bomb! It was the first time I stood in the front of the line, and the first time I was exposed to styles like Horton technique and ballet. I even fell during the audition. I had this serious look on my face, dancing so intently, and then I fell with a big smile. But then I got a letter that I was accepted!

The highlight of my dance life, to date, is the recognition I've received for the Bay Area International Deaf Dance Festival. It is hard for the Deaf community to be recognized for our culture, art, and spirit. The festival is bigger than me. I want the Deaf dance community to grow because if they grow, I grow too. With the Deaf Dance Festival, I basically tried to create a platform for Deaf people. Deaf dance artists have come from 20 different countries to participate, so I changed the name to the Bay Area International Deaf Dance Festival.

Participants all say it's a miraculous experience to work with a Deaf director who knows how to give them what they need and who appreciates their work. A lot of time, Deaf dance artists don't get what they need. For example, some people who have come to the festival talk about how they've had to dance on carpet, which is not ideal for a Deaf dancer. Sometimes they've been in situations where the lighting designer decides what to do without their direction. It can be frustrating. When they get here, they're so inspired to work with a director who understands. They feel welcome, safe, inspired, and respected.

The festival has grown every year. It happens every summer in August. This past year was our sixth year and we had 53 artists. They come from all over the world, and they bring their own cultures and sign languages.

How would you describe your current dance practice?

I dance seven days a week. I practice ballet, modern, jazz, and African, and I also find ways to incorporate ASL. That's helped me develop a vocabulary to give both Deaf and hearing audiences a way to enter the work together. I have been working on this for the past 11 years, figuring out the common denominator for everyone to understand each other. I not only dance but am also an actor and write scripts too.

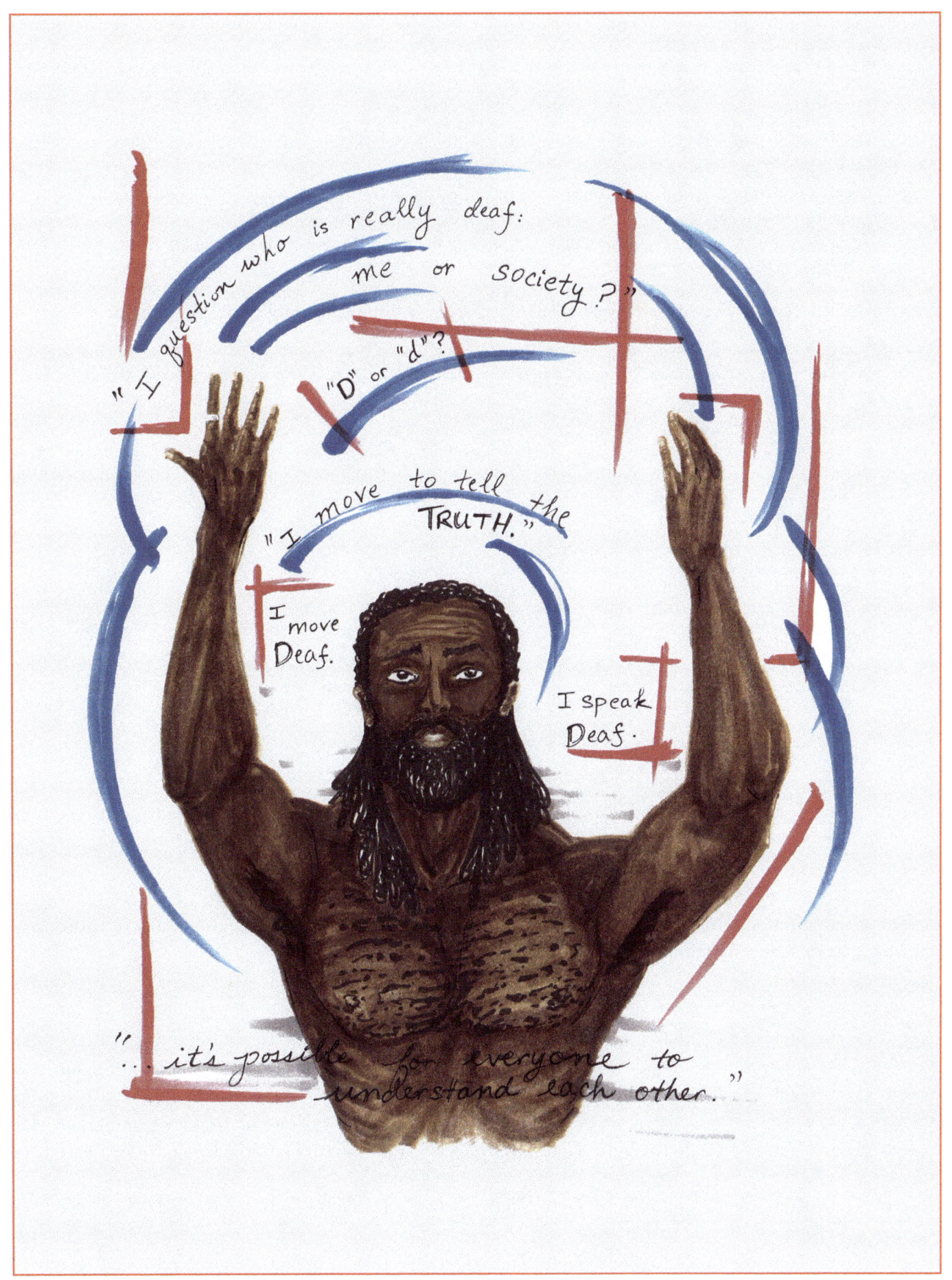

In my choreography, I try to give a sense of what's happening in the world. For example, most people don't know a lot about or don't want to talk about what it's like to be Deaf in prison. If you're Deaf and arrested, you might not have access to an interpreter to find out exactly what you're accused of. In prison, hearing people often have access to telephones, but this isn't the case if you're Deaf. Also, prison guards don't understand how to communicate with Deaf prisoners, and subsequently punish them for insubordination. It's not an easy thing to talk about, but society needs to know what's going on.

My most recent show was about Deaf women of color and the #MeToo movement. The cast was 98 percent Deaf women of color. We don't just dance for entertainment. We also address social justice issues.

I also teach dance in the public schools and at different studios. I go across the country to teach children and adults, as well as teachers, how to teach not only to Deaf students but also to people with unique challenges. I want people to be included. That's my biggest passion because dance saved my life. In high school, I felt very suicidal because I was isolated. But then I poured myself into dance and that gave me a way to communicate with the world. I want to help pass on those tools.

When you tell people you are a dancer, what are the most common reactions you receive?

Times are changing, and people are beginning to see that Deaf people can dance. But I do remember when people used to say Deaf people couldn't dance. People would say, "They need to hear the music." The reality is: We all have hearts. We all have feelings. Art is expression. Music is art. If someone has something to express, we're going to feel it.

I do feel the vibrations sometimes, but if I'm jumping, I can't feel them. That's another stereotype, that we can feel the vibrations. Yes, it's true we can sometimes feel the vibrations, but if I'm doing a double pirouette, a jump, or a roll, I don't feel any vibrations. I have to create my own internal music to stay with the timing, and it's not an easy thing to do. It takes practice and confidence. People assume I have some hearing because I can dance and speak, but I have zero hearing. Sometimes people don't believe me, so I question who is really deaf: me or society.

Another stereotype is people assume Deaf people can read lips. If you're trying to read lips, "m" and "b" look very similar, for example. It's easy to misunderstand; it's 95 percent guessing.

> "I often meet people from different countries and it doesn't matter if they can hear or not. I move my body and I communicate. All the different cultures can be adapted through the body.

What are some ways people discuss dance with regards to disability that you feel carry problematic implications or assumptions?

In Deaf culture, many people don't consider Deafness a disability, though some do. For me, Deaf culture is practically my DNA. I move Deaf. I speak Deaf.

In Deaf culture, the "D" is capitalized. If people don't know sign language and want to communicate, they should be brave enough to hire an interpreter and not look for an easy way out. They should also understand that when the interpreter speaks, their voice still belongs to the Deaf person. Lots of times people compliment the interpreter, not the Deaf person.

I think it's possible for everyone to understand each other. It shouldn't matter what language we use. I often meet people from different countries and it doesn't matter if they can hear or not. I move my body and I communicate. All the different cultures can be adapted through the body.

I don't mind when people call me inspirational. What I'm trying to do is bring the world together. I grew up segregated and alone, and I don't want anyone to deal with that. I could have ended my life so many times but I would have missed all these wonderful opportunities.

Do you believe there are adequate training opportunities for dancers with disabilities? If not, what areas would you specifically like to see improved?

I don't believe there are enough training opportunities for Deaf people at all. When they come to take my class, they breathe deep like they just came out from being under water. They can finally understand what's happening in the class because I sign. Even if they don't know ASL, there is that connection. I feel humble and grateful when I'm teaching. We need more Deaf dance teachers, so I'm currently teaching my dancers how to teach as well.

Would you like to see disability in dance assimilated into the mainstream?

I would love to see that! That is one of my big goals, to create more opportunities for Deaf dancers here in the Bay Area. I'm pushing three of my Deaf dancers to teach, choreograph, and produce. There are so many dancers who come up to me and say, "Hey I want to join a dance company." Deaf dancers feel like they can't go anywhere.

What is your preferred term for the field?

Deaf N' Dance. I actually wanted to call the festival that to signal that we are both Deaf and we dance. I was knocking on doors to say that we need a festival for Deaf dance artists, but a lot of theaters said, "Who wants to watch Deaf dancers?" Some would say, "I know you can dance, Antoine, but can they?" I was told that I was wasting my time. I will be honest: I almost started to believe it, but I made it happen.

In your perspective, is the field improving with time?

For a long time, I was the only Deaf dancer around. Now, when I go to a dance studio like Shawl-Anderson in Berkeley, people at the front desk say, "Good morning," and "Don't forget to sign in" in sign language. People in general are more willing to write things down and communicate.

Because of the Deaf Dance Festival, I feel like there are many more Deaf dance artists. Last year, there were 53 Deaf dancers and choreographers from all over the world. And after the artists leave, they want to create similar events in their own countries. I've helped start events in Turkey, Colombia, and Brazil. I started and hosted the San Diego Deaf Dance Festival, and we donated all the money to San Diego schools with Deaf children. Next year I hope to work with Deaf dancers in Africa.

But when it's all over, it can still feel lonely. When you have another Deaf person to take dance classes with, it can be a major feeling of gratitude and happiness. I have an amazing assistant who is Deaf, Zahna Simon. She has shared so much with me.

If I see other Deaf people doing their art, I can learn from them. If they grow, I grow. My community is growing.

Erik Ferguson

Erik Ferguson is an anti-virtuoso movement artist in Portland, Oregon, and co-founder of Wobbly Dance. He studied improvisation with Alito Alessi in Trier, Germany in 2003 and has performed and taught DanceAbility and contact improvisation throughout the Pacific Northwest, as well as in the United Kingdom, Oaxaca, and British Columbia. He also studied improvisation with Deborah Hay and Barbara Dilley. He is a student of butoh and has studied with Akira Kasai, Koichi and Hiroko Tamano, Mizu Desierto, and others. His performances explore themes of embodiment, gender identity, and extremes of human emotion.

"Dancing is How the Body Learns"
This interview was conducted by Emmaly Wiederholt in February 2020

How did you get into dance and what have been some highlights in your dance history?

I got my start in dance in 2003 when I met Alito Alessi. He was doing a DanceAbility workshop, which is based on improvisation, where I was going to college. I almost didn't go but went on a whim. I felt very shy. I was a wallflower and never danced, not even at family weddings, but there was a moment when my body made a choice. I was really surprised. I became fascinated by improvisation and started doing solos in my living room. Alito invited me to do the teacher training the same year in Trier, Germany, in 2003.

After that, I learned about contact improvisation and started going to jams. I met key figures in the fringe dance scene. I ran into Karen Nelson at a jam, and she made it possible for me to go to the Seattle Festival of Dance Improvisation. There I met Yulia, who would become my wife. We later did an AXIS Dance Company training together. Once the ball got rolling, it didn't stop for quite a while.

I found out about butoh from photographs. I noticed that some of the postures looked like the postures my body takes with the condition I have. It piqued my interest. Obviously, something like ballet wasn't inspiring to me for any number of reasons. When I saw stereotypical butoh postures, it looked to me like the gait of people with cerebral palsy.

The first butoh workshop I went to was with Eiko and Koma. They came to Portland as part of the Time-Based Art Festival and did a workshop at a performance space in a historic building. I literally left my wheelchair and climbed steps to join the workshop, but once I arrived, I found the material accessible. I didn't have to do a lot of adaptation; it felt natural.

About 12 years ago, Yulia and I started collaborating with Mizu Desierto, who runs a project called Water in the Desert. She focuses on Japanese contemporary dance and organizes a program called Butoh College, which brings in international teachers each year. We were studying with her and she invited us to do a piece. It started a long partnership which has included many performances.

Yulia and I didn't operate in disability dance environments for a long time. We were operating in the improv or alternative dance scene. Eventually, we decided to form a company with just the two of us, called Wobbly.

It took me a long time to come to disability culture. I'm one of the three founders of the Disability Art and Culture Project in Portland, but for a long time, I didn't want to be associated with disability. I eventually became friends with well-known people in the disability field, one of whom is Petra Kuppers. She told me that she was triggered when I talked about disability culture as a place of lack. There's the stereotype that it's provincial but it's actually a huge world of professional work. I came around about 10 years ago.

How would you describe your current dance practice?

Wobbly has been hibernating for a while. My entire art practice now is centered on survival. When you have a disability to the extent that my wife and I do, daily needs are fought for. It gets harder to make art in a traditional sense, but I feel like we're living in an artistic way in terms of our surroundings, the people we associate with, and what we talk about.

Even though I'm in my 40s, I feel like I'm having the experience some dancers have in their 60s or 70s. I was capable of lots of movements; I could do contact improv lifts, rolls, and balances, and get in and out of my chair and across the floor. Over the past five

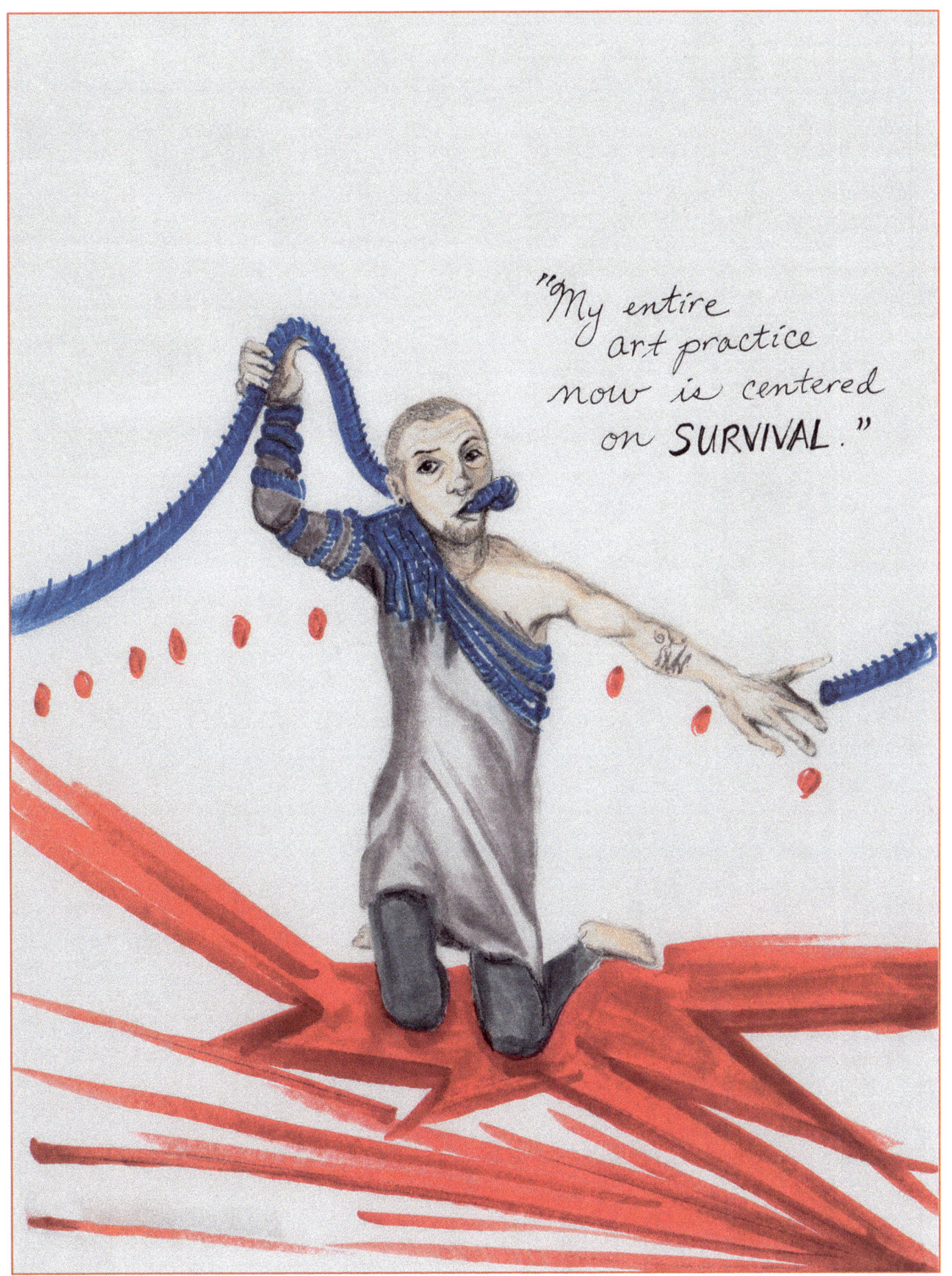

years or so, I've become more immobile. I get up in the morning and call myself a dancer, but sometimes I say I used to be a dancer. It's a hard question for me to answer.

When you tell people you are a dancer, what are the most common reactions you receive?

Here's one of my favorite stories about this: In 2004, I travelled to teach DanceAbility with a friend in Oaxaca at a rehabilitation center in a town of 1,400. We figured out how to travel cheaply by flying into Mexico City and then sitting on a bus for 26 hours. We were coming back to Mexico City after being on the bus and were going through customs. I would have told the customs officer, "We're coming back from vacation," or "We were visiting a friend." But my friend said that we were coming back from teaching dance classes. The customs guy laughed this super hardy laugh at the idea of a blind guy and a guy in a wheelchair teaching dance. But that's the reaction people have, especially if you're not a big-built paraplegic in a sporty wheelchair.

That happens even now. Yulia and I did a choreography project last summer with people who have developmental and intellectual disabilities. While we were doing some blocking onstage, this woman in the choir ran to the director and told him she was worried the wheelchairs wouldn't fit in with the rest of the dancers. The director turned around, cocked his eyebrow at us, and responded, "Well, they are the choreographers." I constantly have to prove myself. The idea that I might dance in a body like this is really hard for people.

> "Anyone who wants to study dance at the college level needs to be able to. If someone is sitting in the corner wiggling their pinky, dance faculty need to figure out how to grade it. Dancing is how the body learns, and people with disabilities need more places to do that.

What are some ways people discuss dance with regards to disability that you feel carry problematic implications or assumptions?

Yulia and I did a butoh piece in a group show with Alice Sheppard in Chicago a few years back. The review of the show said the performers were delightful except us, which described our piece along the lines of "less than delightful and scared all the children." The other performers were doing uplifting and athletic stuff with their wheelchairs and crutches. In contrast, we did a durational creepy performance that wasn't digestible as appropriate disability expression in that context.

The other struggle is that reviewers want to know what our disabilities are. Yulia and I usually respond, "We never answer that question on the first date." They want to center the diagnosis, and I want to know what they want to do with that medical information.

Instead, look at the art. Ask how it makes you feel. What are the colors? What is the speed? What is the lighting? Did you feel annoyed? It's okay to feel annoyed. Just because there's a wheelchair doesn't mean you have to like everything. Just look at the art for what it is. Don't be afraid to laugh or cry. And if someone gets offended, too bad.

My friend, Rhona Coughlin, is a dancer in Ireland, and she doesn't get offended easily. She heard someone wanted their money back after a performance she gave, and she went to talk to the person. They told her they didn't pay to watch a disabled person drag themselves around on the floor. I might have been upset by that, but she told them, "Look, you came out, you tried it, you paid your money, you didn't like it. Too bad. Go home."

Do you believe there are adequate training opportunities for dancers with disabilities? If not, what areas would you specifically like to see improved?

There absolutely are not enough training opportunities for people with disabilities and there need to be more. Yulia was able to go to college for dance, which I find phenomenal. It was made possible by one faculty member making the curriculum work for her. Without that one individual working as an advocate and advisor, she would have been pushed out. Anyone who wants to study dance at the college level needs to be able to. If someone is sitting in the corner wiggling their pinky, dance faculty need to figure out how to grade it. Dancing is how the body learns, and people with disabilities need more places to do that.

Would you like to see disability in dance assimilated into the mainstream?

I think it totally depends on the person and their individual aspirations, abilities, and disabilities. There are certainly people out there with disabilities who potentially could go to an elite ballet school, and then there's me who's not particularly interested. In the mainstream, dance is considered an exceptional and exquisite way of training the body. There are certainly people with disabilities who can take part in that. And then there's this whole fringe side, like standing in a room, breathing, and moving tiny. There has to be more of all of it.

There's a quote by Tatsumi Hijikata *[one of the founders of butoh]* that says, "Only when, despite having a normal, healthy body, you come to wish that you were disabled or had been born disabled, do you take your first step in butoh." He was fascinated with the movement of people with disabilities. Whether that's tokenization, I don't know. When I took a workshop with Akira Kasai, I asked him if I was the first person with a disability to come to his class, and he said, "Oh no," like I wasn't that special.

What is your preferred term for the field?

I fluctuate between a few terms. "Mixed abilities dance" can be confusing because it's not clear if it's dance for all ages or experience levels. "Mixed with what?" is one of the criticisms of the term. I don't hear "adaptive" dance as much, but I don't like it because it sounds like occupational therapy. "Inclusive dance" has the same problems as "mixed abilities"; who is being included? The term "physically integrated dance" I first heard around AXIS, but one of the things I struggled with when I studied there was their discomfort around working with people with intellectual disabilities. I'm curious what they would say today, as this was years ago.

Accessibility that includes cognitive and developmental disability is the last frontier of the disability justice movement. The last piece Yulia and I choreographed was solely on people with intellectual disabilities. It was an original rock opera through an organization called PHAME. They hired us to set choreography on 10 people with developmental disabilities. The experience made me realize how in my head I am about improv. This is not to say there should or shouldn't be complexity of thought, but I learned a lot about how to teach improv to people who don't process information the same way I do.

In your perspective, is the field improving with time?

Little by little, you can see changes. Rodney Bell performed on *So You Think You Can Dance* in 2011. Things like that come up more often where you can see people with disabilities in mainstream settings. But it's just one type of polished mainstream dance. As for me, I don't do mainstream dance, so part of me doesn't care.

YULIA ARAKELYAN

Yulia Arakelyan *is a Portland based performance artist who earned a BA in Dance from the University of Washington and additionally studied with Candoco, Diego Piñón, Jurg Koch, Sheri Brown, Mizu Desierto, Miguel Gutierrez, and Yukio Suzuki. Along with partner Erik Ferguson, Yulia founded Wobbly Dance in 2006, a multidisciplinary performance project currently focused on creating dance films. As an educator, Yulia was a regular guest teacher at the annual Integrated Dance Summer Intensive at the University of Washington, and has also taught at Patrick Lynch Elementary School, Polaris Dance Institute, Echo Theater Company, Butoh College, and Beaumont College.*

"It's Not 'Despite,' It's Because Of Our Unique Bodies"
This interview was conducted by Emmaly Wiederholt via email in January 2019

How did you get into dance and what have been some highlights in your dance history?

After high school, I went to a community college in Seattle for two years and took theater classes every term. Through theater, I realized I really like moving onstage and decided that I wanted to dance. I started to search online for integrated dance companies. I didn't quite know what search terms to use, and I must have tried everything. To my surprise, there was so much info out there: disabled dancers and companies are all over the world! Through that research, I learned about Light Motion Dance in Seattle. I went to one of their performances and afterwards went up to Charlene and asked if she would teach me to dance. That was in 2003. I have been dancing, moving, and performing since.

Through dance, I found community and discovered disability culture. I have met amazing friends and artists. It was also through dance that I met my partner of 12 years, Erik Ferguson. Dance has allowed me to travel nationally and internationally. With Wobbly – the multidisciplinary performance project Erik and I founded – I am so grateful to have such an incredibly strong and creative team of collaborators: Jenny Ampersand (costume/set designer), Ian Lucero (cinematographer), Nathan H.G. (actor, dancer, stage and rehearsal manager, lighting designer) and Sweetmeat (musicians). We have been collaborating for more than four years and together we have created two short dance films, several performances, and a promo video. It's amazing to me that these people believe in Wobbly's vision and want to help our vision become a reality!

How would you describe your current dance practice?

Recently, I have been focused on training to become a software engineer and it has taken up all my time and energy. I'm not changing careers, but I am adding a career that is interesting to me and that can financially support my art career. Wobbly recently finished our second dance film, *Tidal*. We were also hired to choreograph an original rock opera with the PHAME Academy last summer, which was exciting and scary at the same time. My body has changed a lot (and keeps changing) over the past several years. I am no longer the same dancer I was 10 years ago, or even two years ago. Sometimes it's a struggle to keep calling myself a dancer when I can no longer move most of my body, but at the same time, these new limitations force me to find new ways of creating art. Wobbly's new film, *Tidal*, was mostly shot with me lying on my back and using my different types of ventilators so I I could still breathe.

When you tell people you are a dancer, what are the most common reactions you receive?

I've gotten some pretty funny reactions over the years:

"How do you dance?"

"Do you, like, wave your arms around?"

"This is a dance class; why are you here?"

I'm sure there are more, but I can't remember right now.

What are some ways people discuss dance with regards to disability that you feel carry problematic implications or assumptions?

My biggest frustration is when people (and you see this a lot in articles and inspirational porn videos) say things like:

"Despite not having arms and legs….", "Despite being paralyzed from the waist down….", "Despite being in a wheelchair…"

NOOOOOO! It's not "despite." It's because of our unique bodies that we are the amazing dancers (and people) that we are.

For press, I would say write about the artistry and creativity of a particular dance piece. Don't focus on, "Oh, it's so inspiring to see disabled people onstage." Go beyond that. Be critical. What worked for you in the piece? What didn't? Write about what you saw. Describe the dancing bodies. But please, please don't ever focus on a dancer's medical diagnosis. And don't ever say "wheelchair bound."

Do you believe there are adequate training opportunities for dancers with disabilities? If not, what areas would you specifically like to see improved?

No, but people in our field are working to change that. For the most part, if you are disabled and you want to become a professional dancer, you are going to have to create your own training opportunities and not take no for an answer.

> " It's not "despite." It's because of our *unique bodies* that we are the *amazing dancers* (and people) that we are.

Would you like to see disability in dance assimilated into the mainstream?

Yes and no. I think there is value in having our own festivals and communities, but I also think those are too limiting.

What is your preferred term for the field?

DANCE!

In your perspective, is the field improving with time?

For sure! There is more visibility now with people like Alice Sheppard and others paving the way. But I do think more can be done to include more diverse bodies in this field, like more professional dancers who use powerchairs, ventilators, or people with developmental disabilities. The physically integrated dance world can be very exclusive as to the type of disabled bodies that are hired and seen.

ISABEL CRISTINA JIMÉNEZ

"Dance is Freedom"

This interview was conducted by Emmaly Wiederholt in March 2020
It was translated by Lorien House and facilitated by Brenda Polo

Isabel Cristina Jiménez *is a plastic artist and butoh dancer in Bogotá, Colombia. Isa graduated from the Academy of the Arts Guerrero-Bogotá in 2014, where she studied plastic and performative art. She was introduced to butoh in 2010 by Ko Murobushi, and has studied with Brenda Polo, director of Manusdea Antropología Escénica. She has participated in various butoh laboratories including, in 2014, a residency at Casona de la Danza. In 2016, she won the Bernardo Páramo prize. She also participates in solo and collective art exhibitions; in 2017, her work was exhibited in Pascual Noruega.*

How did you get into dance and what have been some highlights in your dance history?

I took my first butoh workshop in 2010 with Ko Murobushi at the Universidad Nacional de Colombia. The workshop was called El Poder Oculto de la Memoria (The Hidden Power of Memory). In the workshop with Master Ko, we jumped, fell on the floor, laughed, and hugged each other. I especially liked the exercise called "the feline," where everybody walked around as if we had one eye in our heads. In another exercise, we dropped to the floor as if dead, and then watched each other from the viewpoint of death. Many of the exercises were hard for me, but I did them the best I could.

In 2012, I participated in another butoh project called *Chaturanga Hamlet* at the Academia Guerrero. We started the creative process with Professor Juan Manrique by drawing on square pieces of wood in black and white ink. Then we assembled a chessboard out of the drawings, which we used in the dance. Each one of us moved on the chessboard like the different chess pieces. We used white makeup on our faces and hands – Professor Adriano applied it with his airbrush. It tickled! Professor Ximena Collazos did our costumes, dressing us in black plastic with red tulle on our heads.

In that project, all the women played the role of Ophelia. Ophelia throws herself to the floor, opens her jewelry box, and begins putting on her jewelry. There were a lot of movements associated with the jewelry scene. Ophelia hides her face with her Japanese fan. We (the Ophelias) said: "I'm crazy with love," and, "They have broken your heart," as we pulled our hair with our hands and ran around the stage on tiptoe. My hair was short, so I pulled it as much as I could. Then we fell, as if fainting, and our princes cried for us. Sixteen of us participated in *Chaturanga Hamlet*. It was a wonderful process. A lot of us fell in love – me with Caliche (Carlos Rojas) for example. In 2013, Carlos and I got more serious, and we're still together.

Chaturanga Hamlet was presented in Bogotá in the Academia Guerrero at the Teatro Libre. I was a little nervous; it was my first time in a theater. But my co-performers and I pulled together and concentrated, and when we entered the stage and began to move, the nervousness left me completely. We also presented it in the Zona T – a street in Bogotá – and in the Teatro del Ágora in the Academia Guerrero.

In 2014, we did a nine-month butoh residency and performance called Odds (which stands for "opportunity" or "advantage") in the Casona de la Danza in Bogotá. We worked with Victor Sánchez, Lorna Melo, Ximena Feria, María Teresa Molina, Nicole Tenorio, Fernando Polo, and Brenda Polo. The training was very difficult. I often got up at 4:30 a.m. in order to get to the studio by 7:00 a.m. We jumped, did turns in the air, practiced the "prayer," the "egg," and the "worm." We fell to the floor. We explored what it was like to disappear into the windows. We experienced the feeling of being trapped. We sweat a lot during the practices!

The residency was hard for me, but I didn't give up. My colleagues helped push me. But in fact, I didn't want to stop. Every day I felt better. I loved jumping, feeling the tremble in my body, feeling good energy, concentration, breath. I felt free. We left each practice exhausted and sweating, but happy with what we'd done. The residency was also good for my work in the plastic arts – I painted two butoh dancers during that time.

In 2017, we did the performance *La Metamorfosis* with a grant from Bogotá Diversa for the group En-Trance. There were 30 of us – different ages, from different areas. There were even some children from a foundation. And a lot of people with diverse abilities.

"We should respect everyone equally. It's that simple; we're all people"

We helped each other constantly. There was always someone to help a person in a wheelchair by carrying them up to the third floor (there was no elevator), or helping those who had visual impairments climb those stairs each day.

We'd arrive at practice and immediately make a circle on the floor, each one of us in a star position (arms and legs extended) with feet touching. We'd breathe deeply together. There were people in wheelchairs, people with crutches, people with visual impairments. It was wonderful dancing with them and learning from them. For example, I used a blindfold in order to move without being able to see. I felt dizzy, and a little scared, but not much. With my eyes blindfolded, I could actually feel more.

We did our first performance in front of the Museo Nacional de Colombia. Later, we performed in the Plazoleta of the Universidad de Jorge Tadeo Lozano. The freedom I felt when we performed in the street was wonderful. There were so many emotions at once: moving my body, feeling the space around me, being outside, and performing alongside my friends. We all felt so happy doing this creative work together!

Our next project is called *El Agujero Negro*. We're going to start it online at first, because of COVID-19. I'm anxious to move again and to feel that freedom again!

How would you describe your current dance practice?

I practice butoh with Brenda Polo. I also draw and make paintings. For me, both are important. Dance is a form of therapy for my body, because it makes me feel more alive, energetic, and free. And then I like to express those experiences by painting the human figure – nudes and dancers, and my life in Colombia. In my work you can see a lot of paintings of dancers, especially women.

When you tell people you are a dancer, what are the most common reactions you receive?

People congratulate me. They say: "What beautiful dancing. I like your dancing!"

What are some ways people discuss dance with regards to disability that you feel carry problematic implications or assumptions?

If I see a person dancing in a wheelchair or with crutches, I think, "These people can dance. They can feel their arms, their bodies." Seeing people with different capabilities dancing is cool. It inspires me to continue my practice.

People who don't know anything about dancers with disabilities might be surprised to see them dancing, but they'll also feel proud. They might feel freedom. They're going to have positive responses.

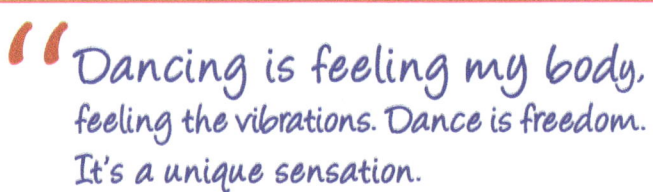

> "Dancing is feeling my body, feeling the vibrations. Dance is freedom. It's a unique sensation.

Do you believe there are adequate training opportunities for dancers with disabilities? If not, what areas would you specifically like to see improved?

There aren't many in Bogotá. I think we need more classes for people with different abilities – for example, those with wheelchairs, those with visual impairments. And I think classes should be for everyone together, regardless of different abilities, not separated into this or that group.

Would you like to see disability in dance assimilated into the mainstream?

Yes. Having mixed groups enriches everyone. I also think that grants and scholarships should be for everyone, regardless of ability, and that everyone participates together. What's important is the person, and what she wants to achieve. People with different abilities and no money can also dance and achieve their dreams with much success.

What is your preferred term for the field?

I don't like "disabled" *["discapacitada" in Spanish]*. I'm a normal person like everyone else, so I don't like that word at all. We should respect everyone equally. It's that simple; we're all people. I prefer "diverse capabilities," or we can call it "inclusive dance." I don't like terms like "lame" or "crooked" either. They're horrible. I don't like the discrimination I feel in those terms.

In your perspective, is the field improving with time?

Yes, there are more opportunities than before, but I wish there were even more.

Any other thoughts?

For me, drawing and painting are like therapy. But dancing is different. Dancing is feeling my body, feeling the vibrations. Dance is freedom. It's a unique sensation. Now that we're unable to go out and dance together due to the quarantine, I really feel that need.

When I can't dance, I feel discriminated against. It's like a form of bullying – it makes me feel trapped, like I can't move. There's no movement in my body, no vibration. When I can dance, I feel space and freedom.

KAYLA HAMILTON

Kayla Hamilton *is an artist, producer, and educator originally from Texarkana, TX and now residing in Bronx, NY. She earned a BA in Dance from Texas Woman's University and an MS Ed in Special Education from Hunter College. She is a member of the 2017 Bessie-award winning cast of Skeleton Architecture, and dances with Sydnie L. Mosley Dances, Maria Bauman-Morales/MBDance, and Gesel Mason Performance Projects. She teaches master classes around the US and received Angela's Pulse's Dancing While Black 2017 fellowship. Under the name K. Hamilton Projects, Kayla self-produces her choreography, organizes community events, and writes arts integrated curriculum.*

"Do I Need to Name It?"

This interview was conducted by Emmaly Wiederholt in July 2019

How did you get into dance and what have been some highlights in your dance history?

When I was about three, I was watching television and my parents noticed that I sat really close to the screen to see it. They took me to a doctor, who told me I have amblyopia. Basically, my left eye was severely near-sighted. In order to see, I needed to get really close to things. Growing up, I knew my glasses were super thick and I went to the eye doctor frequently, but I didn't realize my sight was different than my peers. My parents put me in dance as a way for me to be active and not feel different than other folks. I took basic ballet, tap, and jazz in middle-of-nowhere northeast Texas. I fell in love with it.

I went to school and got my bachelor's degree in Dance. Immediately after undergrad, I produced my own concert before I moved to Washington, D.C. It wasn't a requirement, but sort of a capstone. I wanted to do something before leaving my home state. It was entitled *Running with Myself*.

I was in D.C. for a few years. A highlight was producing another show called *Shift: Choreographers Taking Flight*. I brought out one of my professors from undergrad to perform with some graduate students. Then I transitioned to New York City, where I am now. Here, a highlight is dancing with Skeleton Architecture, a group of Black female and gender-nonconforming performing artists. Another highlight was winning a Bessie award for outstanding performer as part of the collective.

Then there was *DoublePlus* at Gibney Dance, which was curated by Alice Sheppard. I shared the evening with fellow disabled artist Jerron Herman. It was beautiful and magical; I get teary just thinking about it. I'm at a place in my life where I'm starting to recognize my disability and acknowledge it as part of my identity. For so long, it had not been until complications started to compile. I began to think, "Oh shit, this is real. There's no hiding behind it."

Finally, I was part of *I Wanna Be with You Everywhere*, a festival curated by and for disability artists. It included writers, poets, and dancers. I choreographed and performed as part of a shared evening with Alice and Jerron. Although we performed separately, it was so powerful to have three Black disabled bodies sharing the space.

How would you describe your current dance practice?

I don't really take modern dance class anymore. I find there's a lot of spatial anxiety with taking modern dance classes; I get disoriented being upside down or doing floor work. Plus, I'm just not that into it. I do take traditional West African dance class multiple times a week.

Right now, I'm focusing more on choreography. I'm interested in asking questions about surveillance and how it strips and heightens our identities, especially in the context of Blackness, gender, and disability. I'm also interested in interrogating intersections of race and disability: Is Blackness performative disability? How do we de-center sight as a primary source of consumption? Are there different ways of using description of aesthetic and accessibility? Where's the push and pull of traditional description? Many descriptions are what I consider to be technical, dry, and boring. I created a piece where I'm doing the same movement over and over again but describing it each time in a different way.

When you tell people you are a dancer, what are the most common reactions you receive?

That's where my privilege as a disabled artist lies; my disability is not apparent. Most people find out about my disability after they meet me.

What are some ways people discuss dance with regards to disability that you feel carry problematic implications or assumptions?

I find that people make assumptions not connected to my disability, but with my body type. Although times are slowly shifting, I still don't look like a traditional standing dancer. I am a larger body; I have 36 triple D boobs and wear a size 18 or 20 in pants. However, people don't associate me with having a disability, whereas someone who uses a wheelchair might face preconceived notions about what they can and cannot do. People only find out about my disability later when we go somewhere and I have to hold their hand tightly. They'll notice and I'll say, "Yep, can't see."

With regards to press, I would suggest to just describe what it is that you see. Take away your preconceived notions. The goal of the writer is to uplift the artist. It carries so much weight in our field. Focus on the mood, the feeling, and the conceptual aspects of the work, not on whether you can imagine yourself doing that if you had that disability. No one cares.

Do you believe there are adequate training opportunities for dancers with disabilities? If not, what areas would you specifically like to see improved?

Hell no! Teachers who don't identify as disabled need training so when a disabled student walks into their classroom, they're not like, "WTF." Here in New York, there's Gibney Dance that supports physically integrated dance as part of its broader programming, but disabled dancers need our own training center or institute. Disabled artists need to be teaching, and not only other disabled artists. Buildings need to be accessible. People who do not identify as disabled need some literacy about what to do when disabled bodies come into the room. And most of all, again, we need our own education centers.

> "I'm not sure if it's necessary to put disability forefront. I don't put "Kayla Hamilton is a Black, fat, female dancer…" You know what I mean? It's evident in the work I create, but do I need to name it?

Would you like to see disability in dance assimilated into the mainstream?

That's a hard question. There must be some level of rigor, push, talent, and challenge in disability artists to function in non-disabled dance spaces. If I were a ballet dancer, I personally would not go into American Ballet Theater, for example, because I can't do what they can do. They have a long history and tradition of doing things a certain way. If a disabled artist can do something that satisfies the demands of the highly codified techniques of ballet or that particular company, then go ahead. If not, why don't we create our own spaces? That way, we can invite others in, rather than trying to enter pre-established spaces.

This happens with different identifiers: Blackness, queerness, etc. They become the only one in that community or space and then become tokenized. This becomes another set of issues.

What is your preferred term for the field?

I'm still figuring this out for myself. I don't like "handicapped." "Mixed abilities" sounds a little crazy to me too since we all have a mix of abilities.

As someone acknowledging my identity, it gets confusing. I'm not sure what's appropriate and what's not appropriate. Which communities use which terminology? I know for myself what I prefer, but if I'm around other disability artists, I'm less sure what to say. Because my disability is non-apparent, I'm not sure where I land sometimes within that community.

I just rewrote my bio; one version says, "visually impaired dancer," and another says, "disabled dancer." I'm not sure if it's necessary to put disability forefront. I don't put "Kayla Hamilton is a Black, fat, female dancer..." You know what I mean? It's evident in the work I create, but do I need to name it?

In your perspective, is the field improving with time?

Yes, I do think so. Things are popping up. Grants are becoming more available and sometimes accept video and audio instead of just being in written form. People are acknowledging that not everybody accesses information the same way. Residencies are also popping up. Curatorially, our voices are starting to matter more, and people are acknowledging we deserve to be heard. I think we are making progress.

Any other thoughts?

For me, having Alice Sheppard in my life as a mentor and someone to look to as a model has been instrumental, especially as I step into my own identity and in terms of my artmaking. She in particular has been instrumental in the push and challenge I'm going for in my artistic practice.

LUCA "LAZYLEGZ" PATUELLI

Luca "LazyLegz" Patuelli *is a b-boy, choreographer, educator, and speaker based in Montreal, Canada. He is the creator and current manager of ILL-Abilities, an international breakdance crew comprised of seven dancers with different disabilities from around the world. Luca has garnered worldwide recognition for his unique dance style incorporating his crutches and arm strength. He also co-founded RAD Movement, Canada's first inclusive urban dance program open to people of all ages and abilities.*

"Dance Can Be Organically Inclusive"
This interview was conducted by Emmaly Wiederholt in June 2020

How did you get into dance and what have been some highlights in your dance history?

I started dancing in high school where I saw breakdance for the first time. I grew up in Bethesda, Maryland. At lunch, there was a group of seniors cyphering, which is a circle where dancers enter one at a time. I had a lot of strength in my upper body because I use crutches to walk, so I was able to do pushups where I would lift my legs in the air and pump up and down. When the seniors saw that, they said, "Whoa, that's awesome, you could be a b-boy." They showed me what breaking was and I got hooked.

We started a club and practiced every day. Initially, I had trouble because of the footwork, so I created my own style based on my arm strength. I replicated the moves my friends were doing without the use of my legs.

I actually broke my leg at my first dance competition. I was rushed to the hospital for emergency surgery and was in a full body cast for two and a half months. I didn't want to dance again. Once I got the cast off, my family moved to Montreal. I was in a new city where I didn't know anyone, and I wanted to create that community around breaking that I had in Maryland, so I started dancing again. It was about that time I realized I wanted to breakdance professionally. I started training hard. I joined a crew in Montreal and traveled around North America to compete in different competitions.

Through traveling, I met other breakdancers with disabilities. In 2004, I met Kujo, who is Deaf, and Tommy Guns, who is an amputee. I thought it would be awesome to create a super crew comprised of some of the best b-boys around the world who all have disabilities. In the breaking scene, it's common to take the best members of various crews and fuse them together to create super crews for special events.

I started ILL-Abilities with Kujo, Tommy, and another guy, Checho from Chile, who released a video in 2006. Checho has a malformation where his feet come up to his knees. I wrote a comment on his video saying I'd love to cypher with him, and he responded immediately. When I told him about the super crew I was starting with Kujo and Tommy, he wanted to be a part.

In 2007, Red Bull had a qualifier for the Red Bull BC One, a big breaking competition. They knew about my new crew because I had been involved with Red Bull on other projects, and they wanted to bring ILL-Abilities to debut at the Red Bull BC One in Los Angeles. They didn't have the budget to bring Checho, so they brought out myself, Kujo, and Tommy. It was the summer of 2007 when audiences saw ILL-Abilities for the first time.

A year later in 2008, I organized an event in Montreal called No Limits, and I flew out Checho, Tommy, and Kujo. That was the official debut of the full crew.

The rest has been history. Tommy is no longer part of ILL-Abilities, as he's focusing on his own career. We were joined by Redo from Holland, Krops from South Korea, and Samuka and Perninha from Brazil. We're seven dancers who represent six countries and, in the past 12 years, we've toured and performed in more than 25 countries. We developed a theatrical dance piece for festivals. We also do motivational entertainment at schools, conferences, and concerts.

Additionally, we lead breaking workshops for b-boys and b-girls looking to excel. We also teach integrated dance for people with disabilities. Finally, we have a training for dance teachers who don't have disabilities on how to work with people with disabilities. We offer all this to make us more bookable.

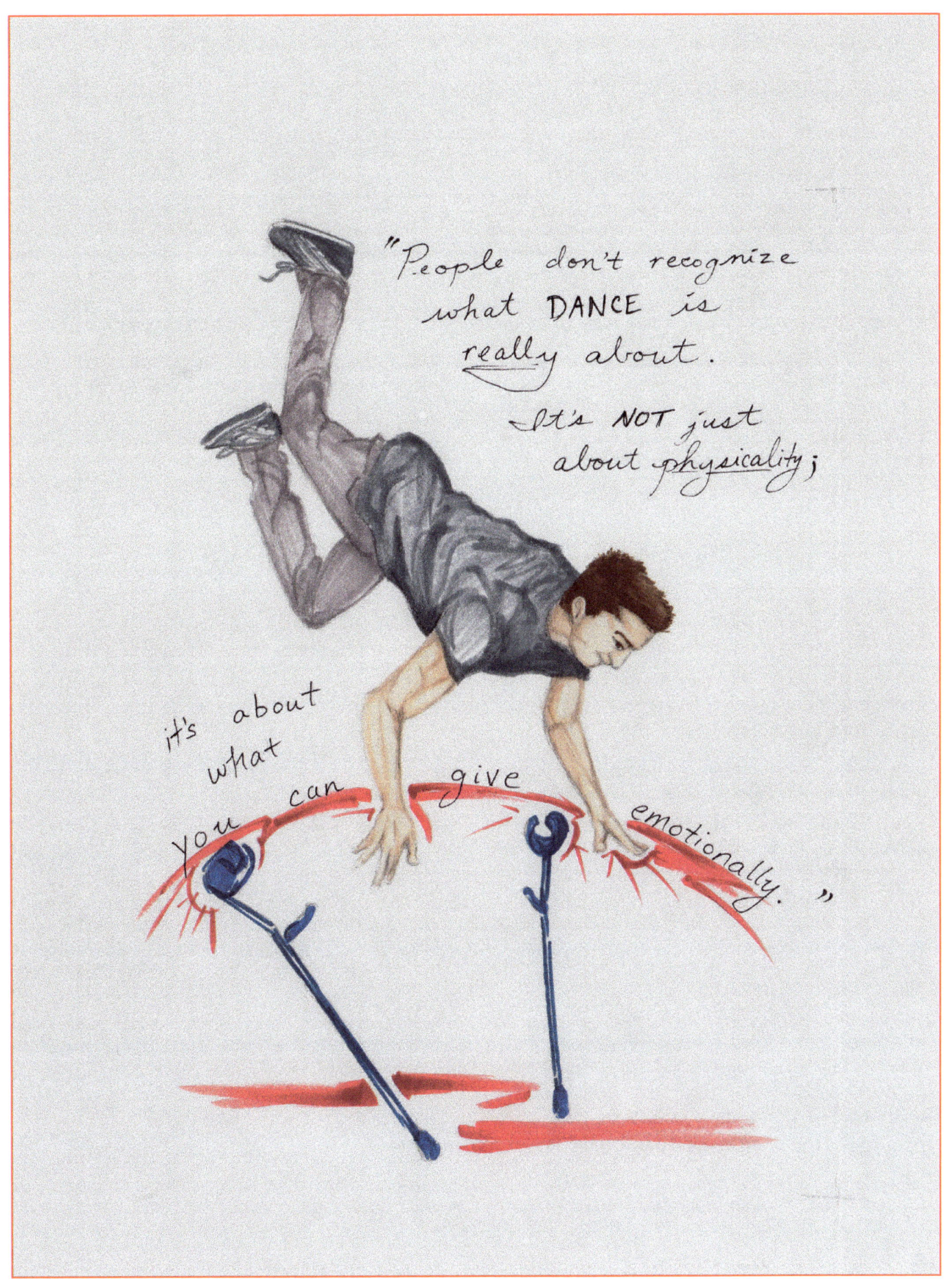

Here in Montreal, I have several programs where I work with students with disabilities who are late-teen or adult with various intellectual and physical disabilities. My goal is to train them to have the tools to dance at a professional level.

How would you describe your current dance practice?

When I was competing more, I practiced two to three times a day. Since starting a family, my dance practice has become more gig oriented. I do a lot of motivational speaking at schools, and I try to give myself the challenge of not repeating material, so if I have a gig on Monday and Wednesday, I try to create a new set in between. As far as touring, in 2019 ILL-Abilities traveled to 13 countries.

I do a daily workout that's about 30 minutes, but it's throughout the day. For example, if I'm cooking and I have a free moment, I might do some squats or pushups. At least twice a week, I spend an hour uninterrupted in my home office dancing or working out. And whenever I'm stressed, I take deep breaths to realign myself. I've learned to meditate since 2017 when I experienced burnout. What helped me was refocusing on what's in front of me and letting go of things outside my control.

When you tell people you are a dancer, what are the most common reactions you receive?

I once had a collaboration with some tap dancers. I showed up at the theater before they arrived and was told by the security guard that only dancers were allowed backstage. I insisted I was a dancer. Even when the other dancers showed up, the security guard thought I was injured. After the show he apologized, but it wasn't the first or last time something like that happened.

Although more people recognize me now, there are still those who don't believe I'm a dancer. Sometimes I'll show them a video of me online. People don't recognize what dance is really about. It's not just about physicality; it's what you can give emotionally.

> "Dance can be organically inclusive. You don't have to force disability into dance. One of the things I appreciate about hip-hop is that it is inherently inclusive."

What are some ways people discuss dance with regards to disability that you feel carry problematic implications or assumptions?

There's an assumption that there's one type of disability, like, "He's not in a wheelchair" or, "His legs are moving, so he's not really disabled." When I hear those comments, I think: Who are you to judge what disability is?

With ILL-Abilities, we never saw ourselves as disabled dancers. We didn't think, "I want to battle the next disabled dancer." We thought, "I want to battle the best because I want to be the best." ILL-Abilities is a play on words. "Ill" means sick but, in hip-hop, it means amazing or incredible, so ILL-Abilities is all about amazing or incredible abilities.

However, the media focuses a lot on our disabilities. We can use that to our advantage to promote ourselves and get gigs, and we can also use that platform to educate that dance can be organically inclusive. You don't have to force disability into dance. One of the things I appreciate about hip-hop is that it is inherently inclusive. Every day is Black History Month. Every day is Pride. In hip-hop, everyone unites to celebrate the music, dance, and art. Obviously, there are egos and battles, but the genuine core is peace, love, unity, and having fun together.

For the media, I'd say focus on the dancer and the emotions they are expressing. Have the disability be mentioned in the second or third paragraph. In all honesty, it's hard not to mention disability because it becomes the elephant in the room. But a dancer shouldn't be celebrated just because they have a disability. The talent and effort must be behind them.

Do you believe there are adequate training opportunities for dancers with disabilities? If not, what areas would you specifically like to see improved?

In hip-hop and breaking, most b-boys and b-girls are self-trained. They practice in the evenings at a community center or during lunch break at school. The beauty is that anyone can show up. If someone is struggling, a more experienced dancer might give them a tip, like, "Try placing your hand here," or, "Lift your head a little higher." In terms of disability, it allows people to just go and try whatever they can.

When I started teaching kids with disabilities, they had difficulty following me. So I started to teach concepts instead, like "This is what a top rock can look like, now show me how you might do it in a wheelchair." My job as an educator is to help students develop their individual movement.

Would you like to see disability in dance assimilated into the mainstream?

It's the same issue as with the Olympics and Paralympics. Some Paralympic athletes call themselves Olympians, while others think of Paralympics as something that needs to be differentiated. There's the need for adapted spaces so that everyone can be accommodated, which is why the Paralympics is a separate event, but for the athletes with disabilities who think of themselves as Olympians, what they want is the same valor.

Assimilation is a difficult question in the sense that I don't think there will ever be a right answer. ILL-Abilities has performed at major venues and festivals that weren't about disability, but we've also been part of disability arts festivals. The positive thing about those festivals is it's an opportunity to get to know each other and understand how our art forms are evolving. It's more of a safe space, because you're being seen by your peers, as opposed to outsiders who don't know what you've gone through. I understand and support the disability arts festivals, but I also advocate for inclusion. If we want disability to be better understood, we have to put ourselves out there and be treated just like any other artist.

What is your preferred term for the field?

I don't like "handicapped" or "invalid." The origins of "handicapped" come from beggars, "hand-and-cap," and "invalid" means "not valid." But the other terms I'm comfortable with. I've been using "differently-abled," but I heard recently that it's no longer accepted. Five years ago, I was using "special needs." I'm not going to lie; I have difficulty keeping up to date with terminology. I start all my workshops by saying that, while I use the terms "differently-abled" and "integrated dance," if anyone takes offense, please educate me and recognize that terminology evolves. On top of that, every country uses different terminology. I was in Singapore and Hong Kong in 2019, and they were still using "special needs."

In your perspective, is the field improving with time?

Europe, the UK, the US, and Canada are making progress by supporting disability in dance through grants, performance opportunities, residencies, and making theater spaces accessible. One of our biggest challenges is when theaters say they are accessible but only have accessible seating; getting onstage is not accessible. People are becoming more aware of that.

Any other thoughts?

I recognize I wouldn't be who I am today without my disability. In that respect, thinking about integration or assimilation is thought-provoking. I understand those who don't want to join the mainstream, but I do. Like any other art that has an underground and mainstream component, we shouldn't criticize the dancers who want to stay in a particular community or the dancers who want to go outside it. Either way, we should be ambassadors for dancers with disabilities. We should be educating and encouraging each other.

JUNG SOO "KROPS" LEE

Jung Soo "Krops" Lee *is a b-boy and DJ in Uijeongbu, South Korea. He joined the breakdance crew Fusion MC in high school, becoming its youngest member. During his first year with the crew in 2012, he won his first world competition, Chelles Battle Pro, in France. The following year, he won Battle of the Year in Germany. In November 2013, he landed on his neck during a practice and became paralyzed. After strenuous rehabilitation, he has continued to dance as well as DJ for Fusion MC. He also performs with ILL-Abilities, an international crew comprised of dancers with disabilities.*

"Disability Isn't Only What You See"
This interview was conducted by Emmaly Wiederholt in July 2020

How did you get into dance and what have been some highlights in your dance history?

I started to breakdance when I was 11. I saw a video online of one of the biggest b-boy competitions called Battle of the Year and said, "Whoa that's crazy." I tried to learn the moves from the video. I kept practicing and when I was 16, I joined a crew called Fusion MC, which is one of the biggest b-boy crews in Korea. When I was 17, I won the world competition called Chelles Battle Pro in France. The next year, I participated in Battle of the Year, the competition where I first saw breakdance, and won. I was one of the youngest highlighted b-boys in Korea.

Later that year, I was practicing a windmill for a competition. I was supposed to do a flip and land on my back and go into a spin. I fell and landed on my neck, and my spine was damaged. My body was totally paralyzed. I went to the hospital and was in a coma for a few days. In Korean hospitals, there is a room where patients go before death. When I woke from my coma, I was in that room. My doctor thought I wouldn't wake up and would die soon. He thought I needed several surgeries to stay alive.

A miracle happened. I didn't even need surgery. My doctor said rehabilitation would take five years in the hospital, but it took only one year. Basically, I'm handicapped, as I will never be cured 100 percent. For example, I still don't feel temperature when I touch hot things. But in Korea, there's a law that you need to have surgery in order to be considered handicapped and get money from the government. So I'm considered a normal person in Korea even though I have a handicap. I don't get any support from the government. After one year in the hospital, I went home and continued my rehabilitation on my own.

My crew Fusion MC had a donation to help pay my hospital fee. Many fans and fellow dancers donated. I'm not rich, so I felt that all I could do to give back to them was get back to the stage.

After my rehab, I went to the gym and danced some simple steps. One time, I played the music for the crew, and I felt like they were dancing for me, so I decided to be a DJ. I loved contributing to the crew and it also helped my rehabilitation. When you have a spine injury, the most important thing to do is give sensors to the lost parts of your body, especially fingers and toes. DJing was helpful for me, especially playing the keyboard. It became a new goal.

I can only dance 20 percent of what I could before. I liked to do a lot of head spins and windmills before my injury, but I can't do those anymore, so I've changed my style. In breakdance, there's a step called threading where you make a hole with your body and thread your limbs in or out of it. I focus more on that now. It's more detailed and not as active.

My spine injury is an invisible handicap. For example, when I'm dancing, I feel like something is stopping me. If I send a message to my right hand to raise it up, sometimes it works, other times it's like something blocks it. My handicap is affected by weather and temperature as well.

In 2017, one of my friends in Europe invited me to judge a competition. That's where I met Redo, a member of ILL-Abilities. I already knew about ILL-Abilities, and I really wanted to join the crew. I felt like the only way for me to give back to all the donations I'd received while I was in the hospital was to go back to the stage, and ILL-Abilities was all about achieving the impossible. I did a workshop with Redo. After that I met Kujo, another member, and they both agreed I could join.

Each show and tour have been unique and epic. After the shows, the audience cries and gets emotional, but every country has a

different vibe. For example, when we went to Japan, we taught a workshop where everyone was really strict and focused, but after our show they were laughing and crying. In Mexico at our last show, people got up and started dancing with us.

We show that dance can change the world. Whether you are handicapped or not, dance is a common language.

How would you describe your current dance practice?

I dance for six or seven hours a day with my home crew, Fusion MC. That includes stretching, free form, and practicing routines for shows. I don't battle anymore, but I teach workshops and perform.

ILL-Abilities and Fusion MC are my family. That's the most important thing. Because of them, I dance the best I can, always.

When you tell people you are a dancer, what are the most common reactions you receive?

"Why are you fat?" In Korea, people think b-boys should be in really good shape. My injury is invisible, so people don't know about it.

It's weird because I am a young person, but I'm considered a part of the older b-boy generation. I won world competitions when I was 16 or 17, which is unique. The older b-boys still see me as a fellow b-boy, but the younger generation only knows me as a DJ.

What are some ways people discuss dance with regards to disability that you feel carry problematic implications or assumptions?

When I got injured, many people sent me donations. When I woke up and finally left the hospital, they said, "Yeah Krops is back! He made it!" But because my disability is invisible, some of the people who sent donations said I was acting just to get money. It made me depressed and I needed medicine every day. A good friend finally asked me, "Why are you giving time to people who don't love you? Don't try to change the people who dislike you. Just give back to the people who love you." After that, I changed my mindset and did my best.

Another thing that bothers me is that some people think I'm the DJ for ILL-Abilities. They don't realize I have a disability and I'm one of the crew. They see me as a normal person, thinking that handicapped people need wheelchairs and crutches, but disability isn't only what you see. That changed when we started to introduce ourselves as part of the showcase. When I tell my story, everyone 100 percent changes their mind.

There are a lot of people who have an invisible handicap, not only in the body but also in the mind. That's become my own mission: to educate people about invisible handicaps.

> "They see me as a normal person, thinking that handicapped people need wheelchairs and crutches, but disability isn't only what you see.

Do you believe there are adequate training opportunities for dancers with disabilities? If not, what areas would you specifically like to see improved?

There aren't dance opportunities for people with disabilities in Korea. Besides me, there's only one other b-boy with a disability in Korea; he is missing a leg. I've been trying to do free workshops for people who have disabilities. I have a contract with an education company. In Korea, people wonder why handicapped people need to breakdance. Since it's very active, they think we will get more injured. Koreans are more open to people with disabilities learning to paint or sing, but not dance.

There is one place in Seoul for young people with disabilities to learn dance, but it's not big. It's a company that works for the government. In other cities they might be able to go to a private dance studio and learn, but there's no specific place where handicapped people can go and dance. I know some Korean people are trying to do events for people with disabilities, but it's still less than other countries.

Would you like to see disability in dance assimilated into the mainstream?

Yeah, for sure. Dancing is a common language; everyone can dance. I am crossing my fingers that there will be more options for handicapped people to dance in the future.

I think dancers in general don't care if someone has a disability. In Korea, artists are more open than the general public. When I go to competitions or events, everyone thinks ILL-Abilities is one of the best crews, not because we have disabilities, just because of how we dance.

What is your preferred term for the field?

Korean uses Chinese symbols to describe words. In English, there is a difference between "handicapped" and "disabilities," but in Korean, they're the same symbol.

In your perspective, is the field improving with time?

I think it all depends on what I do. If I make a good path, maybe things will change. We don't have much history with disability in Korea. I hope handicapped people will see me, and then maybe they will change their mind and start to dance. I really want to show people that anything is possible, but Korea isn't open yet.

Since I wasn't born with a disability, I wasn't interested in handicapped people until I got injured. I thought everyone could access dance and had good opportunities. Now I know that handicapped people don't have many systems to support them. My goal is to make more opportunities.

Any other thoughts?

While sometimes I get depressed about my dancing because I can't do what I did before, I'm trying to do my best professionally. I'm trying to show people that anything is possible, but it's still hard for handicapped people in Korea. I'm crossing my fingers that we will overcome this situation.

REDOUAN "REDO" AIT CHITT

Redouan "Redo" Ait Chitt *is a professional b-boy and motivational speaker based in the Netherlands. He has performed in breakdance competitions and events around the world. In 2010, he joined ILL-Abilities, an international breakdance crew comprised of dancers with disabilities. He premiered his solo show* REDO *in 2018 and, in 2019, made history by being awarded The Swan, the most prestigious dance award in the Netherlands. He was the first hip-hop dancer, autodidact, and person with a disability to win the award.* Redo *continues to perform in theater and TV productions, as well as give workshops and lectures.*

"I Want to Inspire People with Good Dance"
This interview was conducted by Emmaly Wiederholt in July 2020

How did you get into dance and what have been some highlights in your dance history?

I started dancing at age 14 in high school. My friend's brother was breaking during lunch. My friend and I walked into the hallway and heard music, and there was his brother and some of his friends dancing. They were doing movements I'd never seen before. I had never been attracted to dance or seen it live, but this drew my attention. I loved the freedom of movement and knew I needed to try.

We asked the guys to teach us some moves, and they told us there were classes nearby at a community center. I'm from a very small city, and there were two teachers at the center from Rotterdam, a bigger city. The fact that there were breaking classes in a small city was rare.

I tried learning the basics, but it wasn't working for me. I couldn't complete the steps as they should be done because I can't bend my legs the same way as other people and there's a length difference in my arms. After a while, the teacher told me to focus on what I could do instead of wasting time on what I couldn't do. He gave me license to focus on the creative side of the dance, which I found later is a huge advantage. In breaking, you get a lot of respect when you innovate; you want to find your own rhythm, style, and form. I had to find my own movements from the beginning.

The class got cancelled less than a year later because there was no funding. Those of us left only knew some basic movements. Most quit but a few of us continued. We went to parking garages and shopping centers to practice. My friend's dad built a shed behind his house for us, and we practiced there every day. I started doing competitions in the battle circuit. I just wanted to prove myself. Soon, I got recognition at some battles. I wasn't winning, but I was moving up the ladder here in the Netherlands. I would get to quarter finals, and then semifinals. I started to become known around Europe. I was training, posting videos, and reaching out to promoters. From 2004 to 2008, I was just building up my name.

Fast forward to 2010, a mutual friend of mine and Kujo's, who is a member of ILL-Abilities, introduced us. I learned about this super crew of differently abled dancers. I had seen videos of some of them before online. In breaking, it doesn't matter if you have a disability. Even men and women battle against each other. No one is put into categories. I thought ILL-Abilities was a cool crew, but I'd never put my disability on the fore, so I wanted to stay away from ILL-Abilities. I didn't want to be connected with anything disability related.

ILL-Abilities had a show in Sweden, and I went just to watch. Last minute, one of the dancers couldn't make it, so they asked me to take his place. I didn't even know them, but I said sure, so we had to make new choreography 12 hours before the show. It was the first time I performed in the crew, and I had never experienced that kind of impact on the audience. They gave us a standing ovation and people were crying. It was dance with meaning.

After the shows, the guys asked me to be part of ILL-Abilities. My biggest dream in dance was to travel internationally and meet as many people as possible, and I've been able to do that through ILL-Abilities. I've danced in more than 25 countries. There are so many highlights I can't remember them all – commercial gigs, videos, competitions, festivals, local workshops, and teaching children with special needs.

A big accomplishment was in 2019 when I won The Swan, the most prestigious dance award in the Netherlands. It normally goes to classically trained dancers. I was the first hip-hop dancer to win the award, and the first dancer with a disability. I did a 30-minute solo piece that premiered and toured in 2018, which won me the prize in 2019.

Redruan "Redo" Ait Chitt

How would you describe your current dance practice?

It's constant. In breaking, we don't have coaches or companies. Everything falls on self-discipline. The pandemic was a reason to just lock myself in the studio and train. When I'm not on tour or performing, I practice five days a week for five to six hours a day. When I am on tour or have performances, it's a little less so I have energy to give my all during the performance. During my practice, I try to create new moves as well as focus on conditioning. Sometimes I just freestyle.

ILL-Abilities comes together to perform three or four times a year, and smaller gigs with only two or three members happen more often. It's quite a hustle to bring such an international team together.

When you tell people you are a dancer, what are the most common reactions you receive?

"Oh really, how?" Sometimes people will ask, "What kind of dance do you do?" When I say breakdance, they respond, "I can see you broke a lot." That's a common joke. People don't expect me to be a dancer. And they don't think I'm a professional. They think it's a hobby.

> " I don't really mind being called inspiring, but I hope the dance itself was inspiring as much as the *dancer onstage*. I want to *inspire people* with good dance.

What are some ways people discuss dance with regards to disability that you feel carry problematic implications or assumptions?

When I dance, I just want to give my best, but sometimes when I dance my absolute worst and don't feel proud, people say how inspiring I am. I wonder if they really mean it. It's a compliment to inspire people, but when I'm not proud of myself, it's hard to take that compliment. I don't really mind being called inspiring, but I hope the dance itself was inspiring as much as the dancer onstage. I want to inspire people with good dance.

Sometimes when ILL-Abilities is warming up, but we're not going full out, people will say, "You guys are amazing," and we're like, "We didn't do anything yet." It's as if we don't have to show what we can do, we just have to be there. ILL-Abilities goes to the next level with our bodies to do things that are physically impossible without years of practice.

When we work with choreographers, sometimes they are afraid to challenge us. The best choreographers we've worked with are the ones who push us. It makes me a better dancer. I'd rather have someone tell me my dancing isn't good enough than give me false props.

I've seen press go wrong so many times. After winning the most prestigious dance award in the Netherlands, I got a lot of press. One local newspaper in my hometown didn't call me but wrote an article with the headline, "Disabled Guy Wins Dance Prize." In Dutch it sounds worse than in English. First, I have a name. Second, why did they need to call me disabled? At least call the person you're writing about. I think the press has a big role in how the public sees disability.

I've always been called "disabled dancer," but I find that information has no use, like "blind musician" or "gay painter." It can be part of the story but shouldn't be the headline. I've done a bunch of interviews that were done right. When my parents read about me and they're happy, then I'm happy too because they are super critical. When that paper came out with the bad headline, my parents cancelled their subscription.

Do you believe there are adequate training opportunities for dancers with disabilities? If not, what areas would you specifically like to see improved?

In breakdance, a lot of the training has to do with individuality and creativity. If I walked into a ballet or modern dance studio 15 years ago, they probably would have told me they can't offer me dance classes. Classical dance styles are stuck teaching a certain way. I hope that dance teachers and schools will be more open to accepting people who are different. If someone really wants to learn, they should be able to. There should also be more training opportunities for teachers to learn how to work with people with disabilities.

Right now with this inclusive shift, companies are looking for dancers with disabilities, but there aren't that many because we had to fight for it day in, day out to earn our place. If the dance world starts offering training with the schools, it might create a bigger field for the future.

Would you like to see disability in dance assimilated into the mainstream?

For me, dance is dance. I don't care where you come from, what color your skin is, what disability you have; it's about the skill you show on the floor. At the end of the day, that's all that matters. I don't like to label myself. I don't like to put people in boxes. I battle against some of the best dancers in the world, and they don't have a disability. I don't want to just battle dancers who have disabilities. I want my dance to speak for itself.

I've been bumping heads with professional disabled artists who have a different view. I was hosting a conference here in the Netherlands called DanceAble. A dancer from the UK and I had opposite views. I had to interview her and it ended up being a discussion onstage. She didn't have a hand, but she said that when she danced, she wanted people to see her missing hand. I told her the best compliment is when people see me dance but don't see any disabilities or limitations. When I walk around in daily life, I get stared at, but when I'm onstage dancing, all my disabilities fade away.

What is your preferred term for the field?

For ILL-Abilities, I find "differently abled" to be the best term. In Dutch, we don't have a term like that. I can see why people would like to give the field a name, but I would like to not give it a name. I want dancers to be equal. In inclusive dance companies, there's often a big difference between the disabled dancers and the non-disabled dancers. Dancers with disabilities who have been dancing for maybe one year get put onstage next to dancers without disabilities who have been training for years, and they expect to all be called professionals.

In your perspective, is the field improving with time?

In Holland, there is more openness to people with disabilities dancing or having jobs. In Europe and particularly the UK, there are festivals being organized for people with disabilities.

ILL-Abilities gets videos from people all over the world. We see people dancing in the dirt of Africa or the slums of India. Unfortunately, they will have a hard time pursuing dance. In some countries, making a living in the arts is already a challenge, let alone having a disability. It's unfair that where you grow up defines where you can go. I hope things will change, but we're a long way.

CHARLENE CURTISS

Charlene Curtiss, *founder and director of Light Motion Dance Company in Seattle, has been choreographing, performing, and teaching integrated dance since 1985. Charlene has taught dance at the University of Washington Medical Center and Harborview Medical Center, as well as performed in various national and international venues. Her work has been featured on NPR, NBC's Today Show, ABC News, CNBC, CNN, PBS, Reuters, and Seattle television stations. Her original dance technique in front-end chair control redefined the choreographic terminology of integrated dance. She is also a licensed attorney.*

"They're Missing the Best Part"
This interview was conducted by Emmaly Wiederholt in November 2018

How did you get into dance and what have been some highlights in your dance history?

I was a gymnast before I was injured in a gymnastics accident in 1968. For a few years after my injury, I walked with crutches and short leg braces. Then I slowly got involved in wheelchair sports, but the idea of dancing hadn't occurred to me. In the 80s, I went to Rio de Janeiro where I met this Brazilian man who had these drummer friends. I was with them when this big lightbulb went off in my head. We were on top of some mountain with this wonderful breeze. They were playing incredible music on drums and I started moving my upper body and arms. I got carried away and had a wonderful afternoon just exploring movement. When it was all over, my friend said to me, "That was a long time coming back, wasn't it?"

When I got back to the states, I started working with my wheelchair on a technique I call front-end chair control. It explores movements with the front end of the chair off the ground. I eventually hooked up with my dance partner, Joanne Petroff, and it all went from there.

There have been hundreds of highlights. The Peabody Institute, a conservatory for music in Baltimore, contacted me in the early 90s to do a project together where I would control the music with the movement of my chair through sensors on my chair and body. Different notes were connected to different movements, which then created sounds. The composer worked with me to design the choreography in order to create the sounds we wanted to hear.

We did so many unique shows. Atlanta Ballet asked us to set a piece on them. We combined some of the wheelchair dancers in Atlanta with the stand-up dancers in the ballet company. We also performed internationally – Russia, Australia, Ireland, Portugal, Canada, and Mexico.

There were three different festivals of integrated dance we were invited to that were just getting started in those years. One was in Atlanta at the Paralympic Games, one was at the Boston International Dance Festival, and the third was in Los Angeles at the VSA Art & Soul Festival. What was so exciting about those festivals was seeing other integrated dance companies because in Seattle, we were pretty much it.

How would you describe your current dance practice?

Things have changed in the past five years for me. I've had a couple of surgeries and my dance time is nothing like what it used to be, but we are still dancing and teaching. We do more teaching now, which is rewarding in and of itself. What I'm doing to stay fit is an upper body workout and stretches, and of course dancing. I used to swim, but not so much anymore.

When you tell people you are a dancer, what are the most common reactions you receive?

The reactions have not changed much over time. There has always been a perplexed look. If I just say, "I do integrated dance," people don't know what that means so I have to tell them what integrated dance is and how it works. Unless they've seen it, they still don't grasp it. I tell them, "You'd like what I do if you saw it."

We did a performance last year and I heard a comment I'd heard before, years ago. The audience member came up to me and said, "I didn't see the wheelchair in your piece." They're trying to say it as a compliment, but I think they're missing the best part.

What are some ways people discuss dance with regards to disability that you feel carry problematic implications or assumptions?

Joanne and I plus another dancer we work with, Debbie Gilbert, used to go on tour through the schools and give shows or lecture demonstrations. I remember one teacher coming up to the three of us but only talking to Jo and Debbie, even though I was right there, and telling them how great they were to include me, even though a lot of the choreography was mine. We decided that when stuff like that happened, Jo and Debbie would defer people to me. We even got in the habit of me giving an introduction and sometimes running lead as a way of taking away the opportunity for the disabled person to be seen as being politely included.

Then there's the inspirational narrative. What disabled dancer doesn't run across that? Over the years, my response to that has changed, ebbed, and flowed. Sometimes I'll respond, "I think you're such an inspiration." I'll turn it back on them. When I was an athlete doing wheelchair sports, stand-ups always wanted to turn me into the super girl who was an inspiration. That has changed in sports because people are more familiar with wheelchair sports. But they are not familiar with wheelchair dance, so people still feel inspired. I suppose it's good they're inspired, but are they inspired because of the dance itself or because a disabled person is doing it? And yet, is there really a difference?

Do you believe there are adequate training opportunities for dancers with disabilities? If not, what areas would you specifically like to see improved?

Absolutely not. Adding classes at the university level would be a really good start, although dance departments so rarely have faculty who can teach integrated dance techniques. There are many dance techniques that are common to both mainstream and integrated dance, such as counterbalance. Still, most of the quality wheelchair dance instructors work in the private sector, typically as part of a professional integrated dance company. Several of those professional companies offer classes on an ongoing basis, such as AXIS in the Bay Area, Dancing Wheels in Cleveland, and Full Radius in Atlanta. Light Motion, along with Whistlestop Dance, offers classes periodically as drop-in workshops or as part of an educational residency in the schools in the King County area of Washington. An ongoing weekly class where students could simply drop in on a regular basis gives dancers the best opportunity to learn.

> "The audience member came up to me and said, "I didn't see the wheelchair in your piece." They're trying to say it as a compliment, but I think they're missing the best part.

Would you like to see disability in dance assimilated into the mainstream?

It's great to have festivals that are all about showcasing integrated dance. Those are unique and extraordinary experiences. But integrating dancers with disabilities into the mainstream is also very important and shows something else: It highlights equality, acceptance, and new ideas.

Integrated dance has finally risen to the level where we can start being critical about it. Some of it's good and some of it's bad. It's not "all good because it exists" anymore. There's finally enough integrated dance that we can start to have critical dialogues, and people who have an educated eye for integrated dance can initiate those dialogues. My husband is one of those people. He's been watching integrated dance for decades and can call it when it's good or when he doesn't like it. But a lot of people who are unfamiliar with integrated dance wouldn't dream of saying it's not good. I think that's an important step.

What is your preferred term for the field?

I don't like "handicapped dance." I don't really get caught up in whether it's "mixed abilities" or "integrated dance." It's not so much about what it's called so much as what it is. They started calling it "physically integrated" to differentiate between physical disability and mental disability. That becomes important when you're trying to advertise for a public workshop, because you don't want to misrepresent what you can offer.

It's difficult to come up with a language that encompasses so much, so we just have to continue to explain.

In your perspective, is the field improving with time?

Of course it is and it's very exciting. However, there doesn't seem to be as many festivals showcasing integrated dance companies as there used to be. Maybe I'm just not as aware since I travel less now. It got to where I just hated flying! There's also less funding in the arts. On the other hand, there are certainly some spectacular companies, both nationally and internationally, doing wonderful work.

One performance I saw in Boston by Candoco Dance Company had a quadriplegic dancer on the floor, on purpose, who was getting ready to get back into his chair. Two stand-ups came to pick him up – one under his arms and one under his knees. One of the stand-ups started to count, "One, two, three" to signal when to lift. The wheelchair user interrupted, "No, I'm counting," and then counted very slowly to test them, "One… two… three." Then they picked him up. This became a tagline for Jo and me for years. The phrase, "No, I'm counting," challenges who is in control. It's so vital in integrated dance.

Who's in control especially comes up in choreography. Jo and I co-choreographed everything. If she wanted to do it one way and I wanted to do it another, we would dance it out until we found the best workable solution. As a result, our choreography was well-balanced. When a stand-up dancer comes in and tries to choreograph by saying, "This is how it should be," they're wrong half the time. Movement that works is obvious, but movement you have to fight with to make it work is obvious too. When integrated dance companies teach and/or perform, the audience can see the equality of the movement and that's the education they gain. It changes people's perspectives.

Any other thoughts?

Integrated dance is an extraordinary and exciting career path. I feel very fortunate to have found my way into the field. It's been so very rewarding for so many years.

Mark Travis Rivera

Mark Travis Rivera *is an activist, author, choreographer, dancer, speaker, and writer. Raised in Paterson, New Jersey, he learned to face the struggles that stem from being Latinx, gay, gender nonconforming (femme), and disabled. He is the youngest person to establish an integrated dance company in the United States; marked dance project, a contemporary company for dancers with and without disabilities, was founded in March 2009. Mark has also apprenticed under Heidi Latsky Dance and AXIS Dance Company.*

"The Nuances of Multi-Identity"

This interview was conducted by Silva Laukkanen in November 2018

How did you get into dance and what have been some highlights in your dance history?

I came to dance like most disabled people, later in life. I began dancing at the age of 15 at my performing arts high school. I majored in creative writing and minored in dance. My dance teacher, Erin Pride, took me under her wing and taught me everything I know about modern dance, as well as how to run a company and nonprofit. She taught me to be a leader and choreographer. I give her a lot of credit.

I was Erin's first disabled student, so she had no blueprint. It's amazing when somebody says, "I don't know how to do this but I'm going to do it anyway so that you can get the training and experience." I remember one guest ballet teacher, Sally Kane, did the most amazing thing for me in class. When I couldn't get my leg on the barre because of my disability, she pulled a sitting chair and said, "This is your new barre, work on this and make it your goal." By the end of the year, I was able to get my leg on the barre. My teachers didn't give up on me; they pushed me and kept me going.

Two years after I started training, I thought how cool it would be to have disabled and non-disabled dancers dancing together. I had no idea about AXIS, Dancing Wheels, or Full Radius; it was just an idea. So, at age 17 I became the youngest person in the US to found and direct an integrated dance company. At the time, it started as a selfish desire to be onstage, but it quickly became bigger than me. Seeing how far we have come in the past 10 years is surreal.

One of my most pivotal moments was the student choreography show in 2010. I was the first dance minor to choreograph, and my piece ended up opening the show! Another highlight was when I worked with Heidi Latsky for a brief time as an apprentice. I learned *GIMP*, the piece that physically integrated her company. I saw possibility in the daringness of her work. Another pivotal moment was when I apprenticed with AXIS Dance Company for two and a half months. I feel like I'm a better artistic director of my own company as a result. I've been a choreographer for 10 years now, and I've learned how to work with different people and to feel confident in my own abilities.

How would you describe your current dance practice?

My dance practice consists of at least one technique class a month. I teach a dance class once a month at Gibney Dance. And I rehearse about three times a month depending on the project. I also take time to experience life. How can I create work if I don't take time away to breathe a little? I just went back into the studio with the company and I reset a piece I created on Peridance called *The Wait*. I was picked for the Choreographic Development Project, and I was the only disabled choreographer. I was one of four people, and my piece got selected to be showcased at their PLUNGE Program. Then I decided that I liked the piece so much, I was going to reset it on my dance company and make it integrated, which is exactly what we did.

When you tell people you are a dancer, what are the most common reactions you receive?

Because my disability isn't as apparent anymore, people don't take my disability into account. So when I tell them that I have my own dance company and I do physically integrated work, they might say, "Oh that's interesting, I didn't expect that."

Disability in dance is gaining momentum and people are more open-minded. Gibney Dance just posted a video on their Instagram of my dance class, and it got over a thousand views and many comments. Seeing what Heidi, Marc Brew, Mary Fletcher, and others are doing in integrated dance is really changing minds. It's one performance at a time, one master class at a time, one intensive at a time, one studio at a time. Things are definitely shifting.

What are some ways people discuss dance with regards to disability that you feel carry problematic implications or assumptions?

I think the big problem we have when people talk about dance in relation to disability is inspiration porn. We get boiled down to just being inspirational. What that does is it takes away from the artistry of the work. There are people who dance just for recreation, and that serves a purpose in the disability movement. Like dance therapy, that's a very medical approach and it has a place in the community, but it is not a professional dance experience. Dance professionals put in time honing our craft and developing our artistry. We want to be appreciated and we want critique that is more than just, "That was inspirational."

My advice for press would be to tell readers what was good, what was bad, what could be better, how we can grow, and how we can improve. If you don't give us critique, we will never grow. We need critique, there is a place for critique. The problem is that dance critics are not often coming from an intersectional perspective. They are not thinking about race, gender, sexuality, and disability in the art of the dance. They are often thinking about it from the white able-bodied lens, which really detracts from the critique.

My other advice would be to avoid focusing on the disability. Focus on the art itself. It's easy to point out the dancer in the wheelchair, but how does that fit into the overall concept of the piece?

Do you believe there are adequate training opportunities for dancers with disabilities? If not, what areas would you specifically like to see improved?

Until we get into higher education, I don't think we are ever going to have adequate training. We need more universities and colleges to be inclusive of disabled dancers in their dance programs. We don't have that right now. It may not make as much profit because of the population being served, but until we get disability normalized in our education systems, we will never have adequate training for people with disabilities.

> "My dance company just happens to include disabled dancers…I'm no longer interested in just disabled dance. I'm interested in dancers who are queer, trans, or gender nonconforming. **I'm interested in the nuances of multi-identity** and how that influences art.

Would you like to see disability in dance assimilated into the mainstream?

Yes, I would, though there are different opinions on this. Some people say: "No, I want my own community, my own sector of the dance world that is just for disabled artists." I was even told by someone that I shouldn't have an integrated dance company, that I should have a disabled-only dance company. I responded: "No, I don't want that, I think integration is still needed." We need to get to a place where integration is not needed and everyone is equal. Then I'll consider just having a disabled-only company. I think it's important that we start redefining possibility. I want it to be the norm that when I go take a dance class, there may be someone in a wheelchair, someone who is blind, or someone with cerebral palsy taking class right next to me. I think there should be disabled-only spaces so that we respect and cultivate that community, but when it comes to training, access, performances, and opportunities, we need to be integrated.

What is your preferred term for the field?

I don't like "mixed abilities" because I think that could apply to any group with different levels of technique or experience. I like "physically integrated." That's what I grew up knowing and that's what I feel most comfortable with. We use the hashtag #disabilitydance on Instagram or social media to get the word out, but "disability dance" doesn't include our non-disabled dancers in the conversation. I would never refer to my field as "disability dance" unless there is someone out there doing work exclusively on disabled dancers.

When I don't feel like saying terminologies, I say I have a dance company for disabled and non-disabled dancers. My dance company just happens to include disabled dancers. If people ask for more detail, the next level of explanation requires an understanding of intersectional identities and perspectives. At that level, I'm no longer interested in just disabled dance. I'm interested in dancers who are queer, trans, or gender nonconforming. I'm interested in the nuances of multi-identity and how that influences art.

When we get disability down, what about race? What about gender? What about sexuality? What about socioeconomic class? What about nationalization, citizenship, and immigration status? How do these factors impact art beyond just the disabled component of identity? Three decades ago when the disability dance movement was first starting with Dancing Wheels and AXIS, it was a group of white people and their battle was how to get disability accepted in the dance world. Now, my battle is: How do we get everyone accepted in the dance world? How do we get disabled people of color, for example, in positions of leadership and power? I like to think about the nuances of one's total identity, not just one aspect of identity.

In your perspective, is the field improving with time?

If you had told me 10 years ago that my company would be around this long, I would not have believed you. If you had told me there would be dance classes happening around the country in integrated dance, I would not have believed you. If you had told me that AXIS would hold their first Choreo-Lab for disabled choreographers from around the country to come together for an amazing experience, I would not have believed you. There have definitely been some improvements in the past 10 years. We've seen more community building at convenings across the country. The future is bright, and I think it is going to be dominated by the younger generation, which is more diverse than ever.

The one critique I have of the physically integrated dance community is how white it is, which makes sense when you think about access to training, grants, or the variety of resources that don't have the same level of accessibility for people of color. I am one of a handful of people of color to be artistically directing an integrated dance company right now in the US. There are very few people of color who are in leadership positions in this field. Integrated dance is also very Western focused. There's nothing wrong with that per se, but I think we should expose people with disabilities to all different genres of dance. I'm always thinking about how I can push disability in dance even more.

HANNAH SAMPSON

Hannah Sampson *is a dancer with Stopgap Dance Company in the UK. She completed her BTEC (Business and Technology Education Council) certificate in performing arts at Kingston College. She was an original member of the Stopgap Youth Dance Group before joining Stopgap Dance Company in 2010 as a trainee. In 2012, she toured in the European Street Arts Festivals Tour* Tracking *and in the UK Cultural Olympiad outdoor tour* SPUN Productions. *In 2013, Hannah became part of Sg2 (Stopgap's apprentice company) and, in 2016, she became a member of the main touring company.*

"How We Respect and Treat Each Other"
This interview was conducted by Emmaly Wiederholt in June 2018

How did you get into dance and what have been some highlights in your dance history?

I always loved to dance, and started taking ballet lessons from the age of five at Miss Virginia's School of Ballet in Cobham, doing my grades through RAD *[Royal Academy of Dance]*. At secondary school, I studied for my GCSE *[General Certificate of Secondary Education]* in dance for two years. I really enjoyed the course because I got to learn about different choreographers and their work, such as Matthew Bourne's *Swan Lake* and the work of Henri Oguike. I then went on to do a BTEC *[Business and Technology Education Council]* certificate from Kingston College in performing arts. It focused on a mix of theater and dance.

I did a few workshops with Stopgap Dance Company when I was younger, like age 13 or 14. While I was finishing school, I did some more workshops with them, getting to know everyone in the company. After finishing my BTEC, Stopgap took me on as one of their apprentice dancers. This was my dream come true. It was an important step to becoming a professional dancer because I learned how to travel on tour and how to teach mixed age youth groups. I also performed in a number of dance pieces. From there, I joined the main touring company.

The highlight of my dance career so far has been joining Stopgap as a professional dancer. I get to go on tour with my Stopgap family, to show our work and to teach children and young adults like myself.

How would you describe your current dance practice?

We work five days a week, and sometimes we work on the weekends as well. We usually take a company class, and it could be based on fitness, yoga, or a contemporary dance form. We have different and unique dance styles in the company. If we have a dance piece we're creating or practicing, we go over all the movement we do in the piece. Some days we teach workshops. Some days it's a mix.

I get my movement from feelings and images. I use those as my inspiration to make movement. When I start moving, I work those thoughts into my routines.

When you tell people you are a dancer, what are the most common reactions you receive?

I'm not the kind of person who would go up to someone and say, "I'm a dancer." If a person does see me perform, and they say, "I just saw you dance and you looked so beautiful out there," I would take that in and say back, "Thank you." But I wouldn't just say, "My name is Hannah and I dance with Stopgap." I would only mention it to someone who I know and feel comfortable talking with.

A lot of the time, when we are getting ready to perform a piece and we're not in costume or makeup, we have people stop and watch us. We had a recent outdoor piece with a lot of people involved and watching us, and those people said, "Wow."

When people do hear that I am a dancer, I think they are really interested. I'm not sure they understand that it is professional until they see us all perform. Those parents of children with Down syndrome or special needs love to see us perform. I have had a lot of people say I inspire them.

What are some ways people discuss dance with regards to disability that you feel carry problematic implications or assumptions?

It's the wording people use that is more problematic. We are an inclusive dance company instead of a disabled company. As a company, we find it hard to explain the meaning of the word "inclusive." We find that people zoom in and focus on the disability when that's not what defines us as a company. It's just a feature. We do use disability, but we're not dragged down by it. People don't understand that. We have dancers with and without disabilities. There are dancers with learning disabilities, like myself and one other dancer. And we have dancers who have physical disabilities as well. But it's not focused on what we look like. In the company, everyone is seen as equal.

For reviewers, be honest and tell the truth as you see it. Review and write about our performance rather than focusing on the disability. A good review is based on what you see, not on the fact that we're an inclusive dance company.

Do you believe there are adequate training opportunities for dancers with disabilities? If not, what areas would you specifically like to see improved?

I believe there are more opportunities now than when I first started, but we do need more. When I first started, there were barely any. Now, my friends are learning to dance and getting more opportunities to study dance or the performing arts. It would be great to see inclusive companies put on workshops all over the world. However, disabled dancers like myself might not be able to get jobs like nondisabled dancers can get. Stopgap puts on workshops for people with special needs, which gives them the opportunity to dance and express themselves, but there are very few opportunities to dance at a professional level.

I always dreamt of working with a professional dance company, but if I hadn't met Stopgap, things would be very different for me. The other dancer who is learning disabled and I require a bit more support than the other dancers. It's how we respect and treat each other in the company.

> "I always dreamt of working with a professional dance company, but if I hadn't met Stopgap, things would be very different for me. The other dancer who is learning disabled and I require a bit more support than the other dancers. It's how we respect and treat each other in the company.

Would you like to see disability in dance assimilated into the mainstream?

Yes, definitely. At the moment, Stopgap is now studied as part of the GCSE dance syllabus. *Artificial Things*, choreographed by Lucy Bennett for Stopgap Dance Company, is one of the six works featured on the GCSE Dance Anthology. Students study the performance and can come to our workshops, and then get more involved with inclusive dance.

We've also got a YouTube channel called Replay that gives people an opportunity to try out Stopgap's company class, inclusive yoga, and Stopgap's repertoire. We've got our youth groups where they might not have much experience in dance and want to learn more. The same with our older group. It's an opportunity for them to have support from Stopgap to learn technique and skills.

This can only be a good thing. It's important that companies adapt to help us integrate. When I did my BTEC at Kingston College, the course would have been too much for me with all the writing, so they adapted the course so that I could do it as a one-year BTEC certificate course, which was great for me.

What is your preferred term for the field?

"Integrated." Stopgap is an integrated dance company because we're a mix of disabled and non-disabled dancers coming together as one. If we draw a line of who we are, we become restricted. But we're open. This is why I prefer "integrated," because it's more open.

In your perspective, is the field improving with time?

Basically, yes, just like I said about it becoming more mainstream.

SUZANNE COWAN

Suzanne Cowan *is a New Zealand based performer, choreographer, teacher, and researcher. She completed her PhD in Dance Studies at the University of Auckland, possibly the first wheelchair user in the world to do so. Suzanne's career began 20 years ago with Touch Compass Dance Company in New Zealand. She has also worked for Candoco Dance Company in the UK and as a freelance artist. Her performances and writings trouble reductionist and essentialist perceptions of disability and present posthumanist alternatives. Her solo,* Manifesto of a Good Cripple, *is an autobiographical retrospective based on her career as a disability dance artist.*

"I Can't Be Reduced to One Thing"
This interview was conducted by Emmaly Wiederholt in April 2020

How did you get into dance and what have been some highlights in your dance history?

As a child and teenager, I did ballet, modern, and jazz. I was non-disabled at that point. I acquired a spinal injury when I was 22. I came back into contemporary dance 10 years after that when I discovered Touch Compass Dance Company based here in New Zealand. I did a show with them in 1999, and then in 2000 I joined Candoco Dance Company based in London. I spent three and a half years touring internationally with Candoco.

I came back to New Zealand in 2004 and studied choreography at Unitec Institute as part of a BA program in Performing Arts. In 2005, I started a master's program in Creative and Performing Arts at the University of Auckland. As part of my research, I made a series of performances that looked at the relationship between dance and disability. I wanted to research how a dancer with a disability is generative around aesthetics. I also wanted to explore the spectrum from the classical body, which is rooted in European bourgeois aesthetics, to the grotesque body, where the boundaries between inside and outside are less defined.

I worked as an independent artist with Touch Compass, and then I started my PhD in Dance. My research, which I finished a few years ago, was based on a posthumanist reflection on dance and disability beyond identity politics. The body is part of a rich ecology of human and non-human elements as well as animate and inanimate objects. This is controversial in terms of disability identity, which resonates from the perspective of a political body, and which can be relevant but also constraining. What is more current is to have a broader conception of where we fit in a rich ecology that's not human centered.

In 2019 I did a solo show, *Manifesto of a Good Cripple*, which was a reflection on 20 years of being a dancer with a disability. I incorporated my transition from one body consciousness into another. Identity is always shifting; who I am continually morphs according to the environments I move through. I'm immersed in the environments I live in, and they live through me. I'm not a separate self that sits outside the world as a fixed person. I'm intrinsically immersed in environment.

How would you describe your current dance practice?

I practice a range which includes somatic practices, meditation, and contact improvisation. During the coronavirus, I explored contact with the surfaces in my apartment. For example, one day I did a little dance in my kitchen ricocheting off surfaces. My practice reflects how we relate to the spaces we live in. During the pandemic it was a contained space, so I asked: How do we navigate the sense of containment?

While I was rehearsing *Manifesto of a Good Cripple*, I danced every day for a few hours. I work on a project-by-project basis. Outside of that, I have certain core practices like Open Floor. Technique classes are not particularly useful for me, but contact improvisation is great. I like to move with other people and I need a regular environment to jam.

Since my interest is in ecology, much of my work is immersed in the natural environment. Just before the coronavirus emerged, I completed an installation piece with my colleague Rodney Bell. It was an accessible walk through the bush in the west of Auckland, and in it we reflected on genealogy, colonial politics, and Indigenous politics, as well as our relationship to environment. With colonization, there's this sense of extracting from the environment. We were interested in how we nurture and give back to our environment, which

includes other people. How do we enact reciprocity?

During the coronavirus, everyone was contained by the lockdown, but people with disabilities are often contained by places we can't go or activities we can't participate in. In that sense, we have a toolbox for how to deal. We know we won't be able to do certain things, but it's okay. We learn to navigate around what we can and can't do and the sense of perceived containment.

When you tell people you are a dancer, what are the most common reactions you receive?

People often say, "Cool," or, "Great," but I think in the back of their minds they are wondering, "How does she do that?" I've also gotten surprise and disbelief. I remember when I traveled internationally with Candoco, I would have to fill out my occupation on customs forms. I'd put, "dancer," and the customs officers would look at me like, "Hello?" There's often puzzlement and a sense of fascination.

What are some ways people discuss dance with regards to disability that you feel carry problematic implications or assumptions?

The stereotypes get trotted out. Journalists are looking for terms of reference that people are going to relate to, so they go straight for stereotypes. It's a combination of disaster porn and inspiration porn. If they manage to extract from me that my disability derives from an accident, they'll hone in on that. I become defined by one moment in my life. I'm contextualized by either promoting a narrative of inspiration or of overcoming adversity. Both are really problematic.

> "I can't be reduced to one thing, like being abled or disabled. Let's dissolve the binary. What I'm interested in is a pluralistic identity that occupies multiple spaces and keeps shifting and changing.

Do you believe there are adequate training opportunities for dancers with disabilities? If not, what areas would you specifically like to see improved?

It's tricky. The onus is on the individual to navigate mainstream education systems. Should we segregate and create spaces just for people with disabilities? Those environments can be generative but also restrictive. Part of the reason I've enjoyed pursuing my own research is I don't have to fit into a mainstream environment. In a dance class, the references are able-bodied and the mode of teaching is demonstrating. Disabled dance students must adapt what they see with how they move. I find that to be a waste of time. If I could wave my magic wand, we'd have programs set up by people like myself who have experience in the field and who have a rich knowledge of navigating the world as a dancer with a disability.

In terms of getting a PhD in dance, someone could potentially follow in my footsteps; I'm not a unique case. A prospective PhD must be able to think and write; you don't have to audition in a technique class. You just have to reach a certain level academically. However, at Unitec, which was a mainstream dance program, the head of my program, Chris Jannides, was open to me being involved. But I just did choreography classes, not all the dance technique classes. I did what I knew would be inclusive. That's the difference between physical dance training and a self-directed approach like a PhD.

Would you like to see disability in dance assimilated into the mainstream?

Ideally, we should be able to join any dance class as long as we're not worried about keeping up, banging into other people, or getting it right. When I take a class, I just engage with the threads that resonate with me; I don't feel like I have to follow every instruction. Anyone can do that, but you need a level of self-confidence. I have my own process, instead of being directed and prescribed by someone else.

For students with less experience, it would be ideal to have someone with a disability lead the class and demonstrate from that particular physical approach. A lot depends on what people want to get out of the class. If you're not worried about looking like everyone else, then you just go and don't give a shit. But that's hard to do since we're socialized to conform.

If a teacher can distill their teaching practice into principles, they can be adapted to any physicality and in a variety of ways so that people can find their own approach. It becomes self-directed with the teacher offering provocations. That process works well in an inclusive environment. What doesn't work is the transmission model where we're all trying to be as similar to the teacher's body as possible. That can be really unsatisfying.

We all can have the experience of feeling wrong in our bodies. Body politics are so messed up: feeling too old, too fat, even too intellectual. That sense of not fitting in is not exclusive to people with disabilities.

What is your preferred term for the field?

I don't like any of the prevailing terms because the implication is that I'm outside trying to be integrated into the whole. Those terms are problematic because they assume there's a normal, and I'm not it. This is an area where we can be creative and find new ways of defining ourselves. I played with that idea in my PhD research. For example, one of the ways of describing myself in the studio was, "I'm a fast-moving machine that eats up the space." I'm not just one thing; I'm multi-dimensional. I can't be reduced to one thing, like being abled or disabled. Let's dissolve the binary. What I'm interested in is a pluralistic identity that occupies multiple spaces and keeps shifting and changing. None of us want to be stuck in the same identity forever.

In your perspective, is the field improving with time?

The important consideration is context and geography. In some parts of the world there's more opportunity, but in other parts there's nothing. In Europe, there have been a lot of disability art festivals and independent practitioners. That's true in other pockets of the world as well, but it all depends on where you live. In places where there's a larger population, there's more currency for a diversity of people to find their niche. But if you live somewhere smaller, there's less diversity and less opportunity. A lot of progress is dependent on geography and in New Zealand it's pretty limited. Right now the arts in general are under threat.

Any other thoughts?

In terms of what we can do with our bodies and what we can create, the possibilities are limitless. The great challenge of the moment in a world recession is to rethink how we do our art.

KELCIE LAUBE

Kelcie Laube *is a dancer with cerebral palsy from Elmira, Oregon. She has been training in dance since childhood and has performed in two companies. She has been dancing professionally with Joint Forces Dance Company (the performance company of DanceAbility) in Eugene, Oregon since 2015 and debuted her first self-choreographed solo in 2017. Kelcie volunteered as a teacher's assistant in DanceAbility classes for two years, and has since completed the month-long teacher certification of the DanceAbility method. Kelcie is also a Horse Management major at Linn-Benton Community College.*

"It's About the Relationship"
This interview was conducted by Emmaly Wiederholt in August 2019
It was facilitated by Jana Meszaros

How did you get into dance and what have been some highlights in your dance history?

I grew up in a small town right outside of Eugene, Oregon, called Elmira. I started dancing when I was three because my two older sisters danced. Later, it became a family thing; my brother also started dancing. I took classes for many years in almost every style except for hip-hop. I met Alito Alessi *[the artistic director and co-founder of DanceAbility]* when I was six years old at a United Cerebral Palsy workshop in Portland, Oregon. Though we only met like twice again in between when I was six and 16, I was a huge fan of his company, Joint Forces Dance Company, and went to every local community performance.

In 2014, DanceAbility started offering community classes every week in Eugene. I jumped right in at that opportunity. Alito was interested in how I move because I have a better range of movement than most people with cerebral palsy due to my dance training.

The following year after I started the DanceAbility classes, he invited me to do a performance with DanceAbility's performance company, Joint Forces Dance Company. After our first show, he invited me to join the company. There have been a lot of highlights. A couple years ago, we were involved in a collaboration with the Oregon Bach Festival and we also dance at the Oregon Shakespeare Festival every year.

Jana: The Bach Festival show was a cast of 12 dancers with and without disabilities. We danced with the Oregon Bach Festival orchestra and chorus onstage with us for an evening-length piece.

How would you describe your current dance practice?

I dance in the summers at least two times a week at a rehearsal or class. It is mostly ballet and modern, and sometimes DanceAbility classes. During the school year, I generally take three or four days of classes a week at my home studio, Junction City School of Dance, where I've been going for about 10 years. Then the DanceAbility rehearsal schedule is generally two, two-hour rehearsals a week. I finished the DanceAbility Teacher Certification in 2019. I don't really have any outside practice beyond that except at home when I dance around.

Jana: Kelcie has told me that she has to have a rest or stillness practice when the performance season is kicked into gear so that she has the endurance to do the rehearsals. It's her version of cross-training.

Yeah, so when it's busy I make time to chill out. When we have a performance coming up, we'll rehearse just about every day leading up to a performance.

When you tell people you are a dancer, what are the most common reactions you receive?

It depends on the person, but I get all kinds of things like, "Oh wow, cool," and, "That's amazing." Sometimes I'm not sure they are taking me seriously and really believe I dance. It can sound like a positive remark but actually be condescending.

My dad tells everyone that I'm a professional dancer, and people say, "Oh, cool." Then my dad adds that they pay me, and people realize it's a serious job.

Jana: Kelcie and I have travelled a lot together and often perform in duets. A great majority of the time after the show when we're meeting with people, the attention is on Kelcie; people tell her she did a great job. Almost no one comes up to me. When people do come up to me, they tell me I'm doing a good job with her. We get this attitude of thinking the piece is about the disability and not an equal collaboration between us.

What are some ways people discuss dance with regards to disability that you feel carry problematic implications or assumptions?

It comes across as inspirational, and it bothers me. Having people who have a disability in a performance shouldn't be a special thing. It should be a normal thing. I've had people come up and tell me I'm inspiring, and I've seen that a lot on social media too.

As for press, I would say maybe limit the excitement so that the work is seen as art and not just as a disabled person. Even for audience members, I would say to have an open mind. In mixed abilities work, it's hardly ever about the disability. It's about the relationship between the performers.

> "In mixed abilities work, it's hardly ever about the disability. It's about the relationship between the performers.

Do you believe there are adequate training opportunities for dancers with disabilities? If not, what areas would you specifically like to see improved?

I think it's mostly that teachers don't know how to teach people with disabilities. It's that, or they are not willing to figure it out. DanceAbility offers training on how to work with all people at one time.

When I take non-DanceAbility classes, my teachers do their best at helping me articulate the movements. I also have had people come with me to class and help me. It's happened a lot though that teachers have failed to include me. It's okay to fail, but the most important thing is to try. For example, my newest ballet teacher is incredible at choreographing in a way that is simple and inclusive but also is at a level of high art.

I tell teachers that whenever they see me do something that is considered wrong technique, they should point it out and correct me like they would anyone. But that's also because I'm older and have more ability to take corrections. But my advice in general would be to correct the student with a disability like any other student, but maybe not correct every little thing.

Jana: I want to add that I've talked to Kelcie's teachers. They've reached out to me, and I've told them to let Kelcie's body interpret the movement. For example, her plié is her body's interpretation of a plié. Just the fact that she's in the class is teaching other students that they can also have a slightly different interpretation of a plié relative to their own bodies. Teachers should teach students with disabilities like any other student, like Kelcie said, but also let the context of the dance form expand to include relativity of different bodies.

Would you like to see disability in dance assimilated into the mainstream?

I would say it is both its own thing and it should be assimilated. I'd like to see it be a normal thing for people with disabilities to go to dance classes. But I also think there are some really cool steps and choreography you can do with different groups of people who are disabled. There is one group called ILL-Abilities who dance with crutches to do breakdance. It's amazing to watch, and as a person with a disability, it's important to be around people who know what your life is like. I saw the DanceAbility company perform when I was seven years old, so I've been exposed to professional dancers with disabilities since I was really young.

So I think it should be part of the norm but also there's something really special about having an opportunity for the disabled community to come together. I say that because, growing up, the only time I was around people like me was in pre-school because I went to a mixed abilities pre-school. That was valuable. I'm still friends with a lot of those people.

What is your preferred term for the field?

I love the term "mixed abilities." For me, I don't like "disabled people." I prefer "people with disabilities" because it's describing the person and then the disability. I also don't like the term "special needs" because all humans have special needs. I guess I'm okay with "handicapped" or "differently abled," but they do bother me on some level.

In your perspective, is the field improving with time?

Yeah! I actually did a final for one of my classes on how actors with disabilities are filling more roles of characters with disabilities. I think it's getting better in the dance world as well.

MARY VERDI-FLETCHER

Mary Verdi-Fletcher *is the founding artistic director of the Dancing Wheels Company & School in Cleveland, Ohio, and has been a pioneer in physically integrated dance for four decades. After starting the Dancing Wheels Company in 1980, Mary saw a need for more access to dance training, which led to the creation of the School of Dancing Wheels in 1990. Also an arts administrator and advocate, she has contributed to the development of state and national programs for arts and disability service organizations. She has worked to help pass significant legislation, including the Americans with Disabilities Act.*

"Blazing the Trail"
This interview was conducted by Silva Laukkanen in April 2020

How did you get into dance and what have been some highlights in your dance history?

I grew up in an artistic family; my mother was a dancer and my father was a musician. I was born with my disability, but my mother fostered my desire to follow in her footsteps. She would tell me bedtime stories of when she and my dad would travel across America in a vaudeville group. I used braces and crutches at the time, and my mother would put together little dances on me and my brother in our family room.

I just wanted to move, and I would break my brace all the time. My parents kept repairing it and finally got me a really strong brace. Then I broke my leg three times. At that point, they told me I had to use a wheelchair, so I started using a wheelchair when I was 12. I loved to watch *American Bandstand* and would groove to the music, and before long I broke the wheel off my wheelchair. Even to this day, I have a hard time watching dance because my body wants to join. If I go to a ballet, I twitch through the whole thing. I did back then as well.

In the early 70s, there was a resurgence of community dances. It was the beginning of the disco days. One day, this guy came up to me and asked if I wanted to dance. I said, "I don't know if I can," but we started experimenting and my wheels started gliding. I was doing the same partnering as the standup girls but using my wheels. It felt natural and unique, like skating and dancing at the same time. It had such a fluidity and speed to it.

I got hooked and started looking at how I could do various dances. I was going to different clubs, and soon everybody wanted to partner with me. My best friend's husband was a good dancer, and we started to partner together regularly. We got very good.

Dance Fever was a competition show like *Dancing with the Stars* that was going around the country. The producer would travel to different states to select dancers to be on the show. I called up and asked to participate, and they took our names down to audition. We showed up that night and they were floored that I was in a wheelchair. They didn't know what to do. We had put together a routine with a smash ending. My partner had been a gymnast, and at the end of our dance he would take a flying leap from across the stage, jump onto my armrests, and over my head. The crowd went wild. There were 2,000 people in the audience, and we got a standing ovation. Looking back now, there are so many more dance moves we could have done, but at the time we were blazing the trail.

We were chosen as alternates to be on the show. Interestingly, the producer said to me, "You know, this was really difficult. If I didn't choose you, they would have said it was because you're handicapped, and if I chose you, they would say it's because you're handicapped." I had never thought about it that way. This was before the Americans with Disabilities Act.

We started to get on a lot of different television shows, and then we were chosen to be on a Walt Disney show that highlighted all kinds of acts. There was even a dog act. I was talking to the dog's mom who was telling me he performed all over the country. I thought, "If that dog can do it, then so can I." She told me how her dog was sponsored by a dog food company. So I went to a wheelchair company, Invacare, and pitched my idea of doing shows and talking about their wheelchair if they gave me a new one, and the traveling would be paid for by their sponsorship. And they went for it. We did 72 shows a year all over the country. Before you know it, we got on bigger shows like CNN and Good Morning America. People saw us and wanted to be a part. Dancing Wheels was born.

At first we were just a dance company that got paid to perform. I wanted to reach more people who couldn't necessarily afford to pay us and go to schools, so in 1990 I turned Dancing Wheels into a 501c3 and licensed and trademarked it. I was connected with Cleveland Ballet, and they were looking to expand their outreach and educational programs. They bought the license to be called Cleveland Ballet Dancing Wheels. In doing so, I told them they had to hire me to manage and develop their program. I worked there for 10 years.

By that time, we had really grown. We went from a small group to a full company of eight to 10 dancers. I started producing and commissioning pieces. I hired Sabatino Verlezza from New York to be the associate artistic director, and his wife Barbara Allegra Verlezza ran the school. They were with Dancing Wheels for almost 10 years. Sabotino did beautiful choreography and had amazing vision.

Dancers have come and gone over the years. Some have been with me a very long time. I have several dancers who I am still really good friends with. Our repertoire has over 72 pieces in it now. It's hard to believe it's been 40 years.

How would you describe your current dance practice?

The company takes class everyday Monday through Friday. Typically, it's ballet, modern, or contemporary, and we also have a conditioning class. Our 12 to 3 p.m. time slot is always immersed in restaging works or the creative process of developing new works. The dancers are full time, so they work 12 months out of the year and have paid vacations, holidays, and sick days. Nobody gets paid a tremendous amount, but it's consistent. The dancers can rely on that base salary, and then they get paid extra for performances and teaching.

When you tell people you are a dancer, what are the most common reactions you receive?

What I love is when parents tell little kids at a show, "You know, she's a dancer." The kids will cock their head. You can see they don't want to be rude, but they don't know what their mother or father is talking about. Then I do a little twirl with them and they start to get it.

> "At the end of our dance my partner would take a flying leap from across the stage, jump onto my armrests, and over my head. The crowd went wild...Looking back now, there are so many more dance moves we could have done, but at the time we were blazing the trail.

What are some ways people discuss dance with regards to disability that you feel carry problematic implications or assumptions?

The number one thing is they think that if they've seen one physically integrated dance company, they've seen them all. That's an issue with presenters too: "Oh, we presented Dancing Wheels, so we don't need to present AXIS Dance Company," or vice versa. I've found over the years that attitude has narrowed the opportunities for touring. Presenters will book several modern or ballet companies, but only one physically integrated dance company. They think it's all the same.

Do you believe there are adequate training opportunities for dancers with disabilities? If not, what areas would you specifically like to see improved?

More and more now, integrated companies are providing training. They almost all have summer intensives. Compared to when I started dancing, there are leaps and bounds more training opportunities, but not at the university level.

We did our first level one certification of the Dancing Wheels teacher training method recently and learned a lot by doing it. We're offering another level one certification soon. I notice that a lot of people in other countries revere our company and our teaching process more than people in the US.

We're always going to be at a standstill at the university level as long as dance faculty are saying it's too cumbersome and takes too much time to teach students with disabilities, or it's going to negatively affect the non-disabled students. It doesn't have to if you know the technique of translation. Ours isn't the only one, but teachers need to understand there are ways to do it.

Sometimes I just want to throw my hands up. I'm tired of preaching this.

Would you like to see disability in dance assimilated into the mainstream?

It is in the mainstream in that Dancing Wheels competes with other dance companies for opportunities, whether they're disabled or not. We're in showcases and mainstage concerts. It's a competitive field, and we participate in the mainstream in that way.

There's a whole split where it seems like the younger mindset wants to put their disability first. They are proud of their disability and want to be known as a disabled dancer or disabled choreographer. But then there are mindsets like mine where I happen to be disabled, but first and foremost, I'm a dancer and artistic director. I never say I'm a disabled artistic director.

I go back to the African American community. How many say, "I'm a Black choreographer"? People know they're Black. Seeing is believing. If you're a dancer, you're a dancer. You don't have to make your identity so in-your-face all the time. But those people have a right to their opinion, and I have a right to mine.

If a presenter brings us in, we're going to put on a high-quality show that happens to have some wheelchair dancers and standup dancers working together. It will be artistically high level and entertaining. For me, entertainment means we impact people, and the audience will have a feeling, whether it's sorrow or joy.

What is your preferred term for the field?

I use "physically integrated dance." It's a much broader term that connotes more than just wheelchair dancers and standup dancers. Our company is integrated in a lot of different ways beyond disability: gender, ethnicity, age. When I explain to kids what "physically integrated dance" is, I break it down. I ask them what "integrated" means. It means being together. What does "physical" refer to? The body. We're all different bodies moving together. And then the kids get it.

In your perspective, is the field improving with time?

Academia is not, and I think presenters are afraid. I think presenters are afraid of dance in general. It's far more expensive than presenting music or theater. Our heyday in terms of touring was before 9/11. Now, presenters want to know if we'll sell seats like Alvin Ailey.

The amount of integrated companies, as well as dancers and choreographers with disabilities, really has improved. They are taking hold and developing themselves. But they are still not a commodity. I go to hire a wheelchair dancer and it's like pulling teeth. And then I often have to train the wheelchair dancers from scratch. It takes a long time to develop a dancer.

KAZUYO MORITA

Kazuyo Morita *is a dancer and actress from Osaka, Japan. As the leader/founder of "Performance for All People – CONVEY," Kazuyo has performed in such events as the Yokohama Paratriennale and Happy Spot Nara, as well as collaborated with SLOW MOVEMENT, Knit Cap Theater, and Niwa Gekidan Penino. Kazuyo also teaches workshops, choreographs, and directs dance performances for people with disabilities. Together with her mother, she launched the nonprofit P'spot 14, which includes a dance studio and produces stage performances. She has also participated in symposiums hosted by the Agency for Cultural Affairs and the British Council.*

"We Need Role Models"

This interview was conducted by Silva Laukkanen in August 2020
It was translated by Yuka Matsudaira

How did you get into dance and what have been some highlights in your dance history?

In my second year of high school, which is like 10th grade, I watched a musical by Takarazuka Revue – a Japanese all-female musical theater troupe. I was impressed and decided to pursue the performing arts. I tried to get into college for art, but because of my disability, I was not able to take the entrance exam. I was told I could not participate in the performance art of dance. That was quite a major incident for me because it was the first time someone denied me something because of my disability. I live in a society where I am not allowed to speak up. That was when I was faced with the reality of being a disabled person.

After that, I got into a non-art college where I majored in economics, which is totally unrelated to the performing arts, but I joined a theater club at the college and after that I started going to a musical school where so-called healthy people were being trained. Back then, there was no place for disabled people to learn how to dance so I had no other choice than to join somewhere that was geared toward only non-disabled people. But that musical school accepted me, and I was able to learn how to dance there. I studied jazz dance, ballet, and acting for three to four years. Most of the stuff I learned was not something I was able to do. But I was determined to learn, and I think it was a good experience for me.

After that, I tried different types of dance. I was trying to find what fit my body, like trying on different clothes. For several years, I was just comparing the differences between healthy people's bodies and my own body. I studied what they can do, what I can do, what they cannot do, and what I cannot do. That's how I saw my body back then.

Something changed in 2000. A director named Wolfgang Stange started offering workshops in Japan. I participated, and for the first time, I experienced free movement with no set style or form. I thought, "Oh, I can move more freely in this way." In 2004, I started creating my own performances.

From 2008 to 2010, I joined a performance project organized by DANCE BOX in the city of Kobe that facilitated dance with disabled and non-disabled dancers. The director was a contemporary dancer. His way of creating dance is very special; the dancers are forced to really look into their bodies when he's choreographing. It's not about form or movement styles. I suffered a lot during that time. I had learned classical ballet and jazz dance, but the director didn't like me using those styles and forms. Instead, he made me partner with a wheelchair dancer. He forced me to explore how to dance with my partner. It was a really good experience for me.

In 2012, I created a performance called *Walking Tomorrow*. I started being able to show how I can dance with my own body and put what I really want into my own dance performance.

In 2017, I created a 20-minute piece called *Our Beginning* with citizens in the city of Miyakonojo. It grew out of a two-day workshop I gave in the city the previous year. Afterwards, the organization where I taught asked me to teach workshops on the weekends for three months. That became the performance piece. There were 12 people in the piece and half were disabled. It was a highlight from my career.

There are many performances like this in Japan, but there is usually no continuation once the performance is done. After this show, the participants asked an assistant who taught ballet locally to keep teaching them. Those classes are still going on today and it makes me so happy. There are more projects for disabled people these days, but most of the time, the disabled people are passive. In this instance, the students took the initiative for the classes to continue. It is a success story.

"It's very important to establish the status of disabled dancers and train more disabled dancers"

How would you describe your current dance practice?

I take classical ballet on a regular basis to maintain my body. When I was taking ballet before, I was trying to get closer to the bodies of non-disabled people, but now my focus is on what I can do with my own body or how I can translate a step. My sense of achievement is definitely higher now.

I started grad school in 2019 at Kobe University to research how disabled people dance. This area of research is not yet advanced in Japan. I have been trying hard to gather information, but there are hardly any research papers on the topic in Japan, so I'm relying on research papers published abroad.

I also started teaching at a university in Osaka in 2020. I have a two-year contract. Next year, the students in my seminars are going to create a small performance piece with citizens, including disabled people. This year, my students are learning about disability expression online because of the pandemic.

When you tell people you are a dancer, what are the most common reactions you receive?

When I encounter people who have never met a disabled person before or who have never seen disabled dancing, I feel like they don't believe what I'm saying. But these days, I just show them a video or pictures on my phone right away.

What are some ways people discuss dance with regards to disability that you feel carry problematic implications or assumptions?

People's comments and discussion will differ widely depending on what kind of dance performance disabled dancers are doing. There is not really a solid category for disabled dance. For example, there are wheelchair dancers doing competitive dance, there's a dance school for children with Down syndrome, and there are some disabled dance battles. It's really hard to categorize disabled dance.

There are some occasions when I have felt disappointed with the press. I think it's getting better compared with several years ago. Back then, it was like disability was something to conquer or overcome. I still see that wording and expression these days, but it is much less.

> "We need **role models** in this field so there's somebody who other disabled people can copy or aspire to be, but I don't think that's possible unless **more dancers come into this field.**

Do you believe there are adequate training opportunities for dancers with disabilities?

No, there are almost none. There is a big nonprofit organization that started a dance school for Down syndrome children. And there is also a dance group for wheelchair dancers. Different municipal governments offer occasional workshops for disabled dancers, but there are not continuous efforts to offer dance training for disabled students.

That is one of the reasons I started my own dance studio, P'spot 14. Disabled dancers are welcome to come and train, but I hardly get any new disabled students joining my studio. It's hard for disabled people to find the motivation to start dance. I recently gave lessons to an eight-year-old disabled dancer. That child wanted to learn dance because her mother was doing jazz dancing.

I personally have a little experience in a type of traditional dance called Shimai that's part of the traditional Noh drama, where the performers dance with masks. I've never really learned any other traditional Japanese dance. I never pursued it because you have to be able to squat and sit on the floor to do the dances. Overall, there is not a traditional dance school that accepts disabled students.

Would you like to see disability in dance assimilated into the mainstream?

In Japan, if you're disabled or not, it's really hard to make a living as a dancer. Something started changing in the past couple of years though; the Tokyo Olympics and Paralympics were scheduled for summer 2020 and are postponed now because of the pandemic. Because of those big events, other notable dance-related events were scheduled, so there have been more disabled dance events and grants in Japan. What I see these days is a clear boundary or a distinction between the Olympic and Paralympic Games. That's also what's happening in the dance field; there is disabled dance versus non-disabled dance. It's quite difficult for people in Japan to visualize what mainstream dance is.

What is your preferred term for the field?

Just dance.

In your perspective, is the field improving with time?

Yes, I think so, but I'm afraid this trend will go back a little bit because of the pandemic. It's a financial issue. Thanks to the power of the Olympic Games scheduled in Japan, it has become easier to receive grants. People are afraid this trend will revert after the Olympics.

In 2019, the Japanese government enacted a law to promote the expression, art, and activities of disabled people. I was a member on the expert committee. The law covers the entire field of art, including fine arts and performing arts. It targets access, training, as well as promotes international exchange.

However, this law is managed by two different ministries: The Ministry of Health, Labor, and Welfare, and the Ministry of Education, Culture, Sports, Science, and Technology. It was originally managed by the Ministry of Health because it was considered a welfare program. When you talk about access for mentally disabled people, you have to talk about their homes or workplaces. If you talk about access for physically disabled people, you have to talk about public spaces. It's completely different. That's why there is the impression that disability access is related to social welfare.

In the performing arts, there are very few horizontal connections between the organizations that work with disabled people because there is no single organization that manages everything. This new law gives grants, but many organizations have financial issues and need more money. I'm a member of the committee that offers the grants. The reason why they chose me as a judge is that I'm a freelance artist who doesn't belong to any larger organization, so I have no conflicts of interest.

In Japanese society, there are still many prejudices and barriers when it comes to disabled people accessing dance. It is directly related to what I said earlier about how to motivate disabled people to learn dance. We need role models in this field so there's somebody who other disabled people can copy or aspire to be, but I don't think that's possible unless more dancers come into this field. I personally think it's very important to establish the status of disabled dancers and train more disabled dancers. That's what I am focused on right now.

Bill Shannon

Bill Shannon is an interdisciplinary artist who explores body-centric work through video installation, sculpture, linguistics, sociology, choreography, dance, and politics. He has been awarded a United States Artist Award in Dance, a Guggenheim Fellowship in Choreography, a Foundation for Contemporary Art Fellowship in Performance Art, and has worked for Cirque Du Soleil. Bill created a specific movement vocabulary through his use of crutches and became a fixture at underground dance clubs for his contemporary kinetic expressions of hip-hop and skateboarding. His singular style of mobility, performance, and dance required multiple new crutch designs to sustain technical advances in his movement.

"Space, Light, Time, and The Human Condition"
This interview was conducted by Emmaly Wiederholt in April 2019

How did you get into dance and what have been some highlights in your dance history?

Dancing was a part of my family life as a child. My parents were full-time antiwar activists and organizers in the 70s and 80s. There were lots of meetings and protests with parties afterward where there was often live drumming. I remember dancing as young as five years old with my brace on my leg. My earliest connection to dance was the connection to music and the fact it extended from family and community.

I do not self-identify as a dancer. I identify as an interdisciplinary artist. I dance on crutches due to a physical disability, and that dancing is part of a larger body of performance and visual work. I look at my work as a pie sliced into different sections. The dance "slice" became more artistically successful than my other pursuits as an artist, though all the slices remain equally important to me.

Back to my childhood, art was a leveling of the playing field. In gym or recess, I was behind or picked last. Art class was a place where I could excel. It became my favorite thing in school. I was also very physically active. I was mainstreamed before mainstreaming was even a thing. My parents petitioned the school board where I grew up in Pittsburgh for me to attend a school where there were no other disabled kids.

In the mid-80s, I lived and breathed hip-hop and skateboarding culture. In the 90s, I started creating performance art with wearable sculpture under the name "Crutch." It wasn't disability dance; it was political performance art. When I moved to New York, I was re-immersed in the house, hip-hop, and club music scene and started skating on modified "rocker-bottom" crutches. I entered competitions where I would dance on crutches in hip-hop, boogaloo, or house styles. In hip-hop culture, you're competing in a context of bravado and larger than life personality. My crew in NYC was called The Step Fēnz (pronounced "fiends"), who I met while street skating. They gave me the moniker "Crutch Master." I was dancing very competitively against other dancers with similar grandiose handles and I considered it over time as an honor. The moniker fit for where I was as a street-based dance artist but was less fitting in other creative contexts. I retired it later when I stopped dancing competitively.

I was around for the birth of the disability dance scene and the early formation of companies like AXIS and Light Motion, as well as for the bourgeoning hip-hop summits, conferences, and festivals. It was a split identity for me. Disability dance was primarily white and doing ballet and modern. I didn't fit in culturally. Then there was hip-hop, in which I was often one of the few or only white or disabled people entering the circles but did fit in culturally as far as relationship to music, fashion, language, and most critically the freestyle ethos of hip-hop. These two worlds had very little crossover. I didn't really fit in with the disabled dance community, and I was also an anomaly in the hip-hop community. While accepted and appreciated by those respective and disparate communities, I never felt truly accepted as central to either.

How would you describe your current dance practice?

My practice has always been about solving problems. Currently, I'm working on the challenge of video art as a wearable medium through 3D printing by collaborating with a hardware coder.

Prior to that, I put together four group pieces that were concerned with the problem of translating the endless cipher of street dance

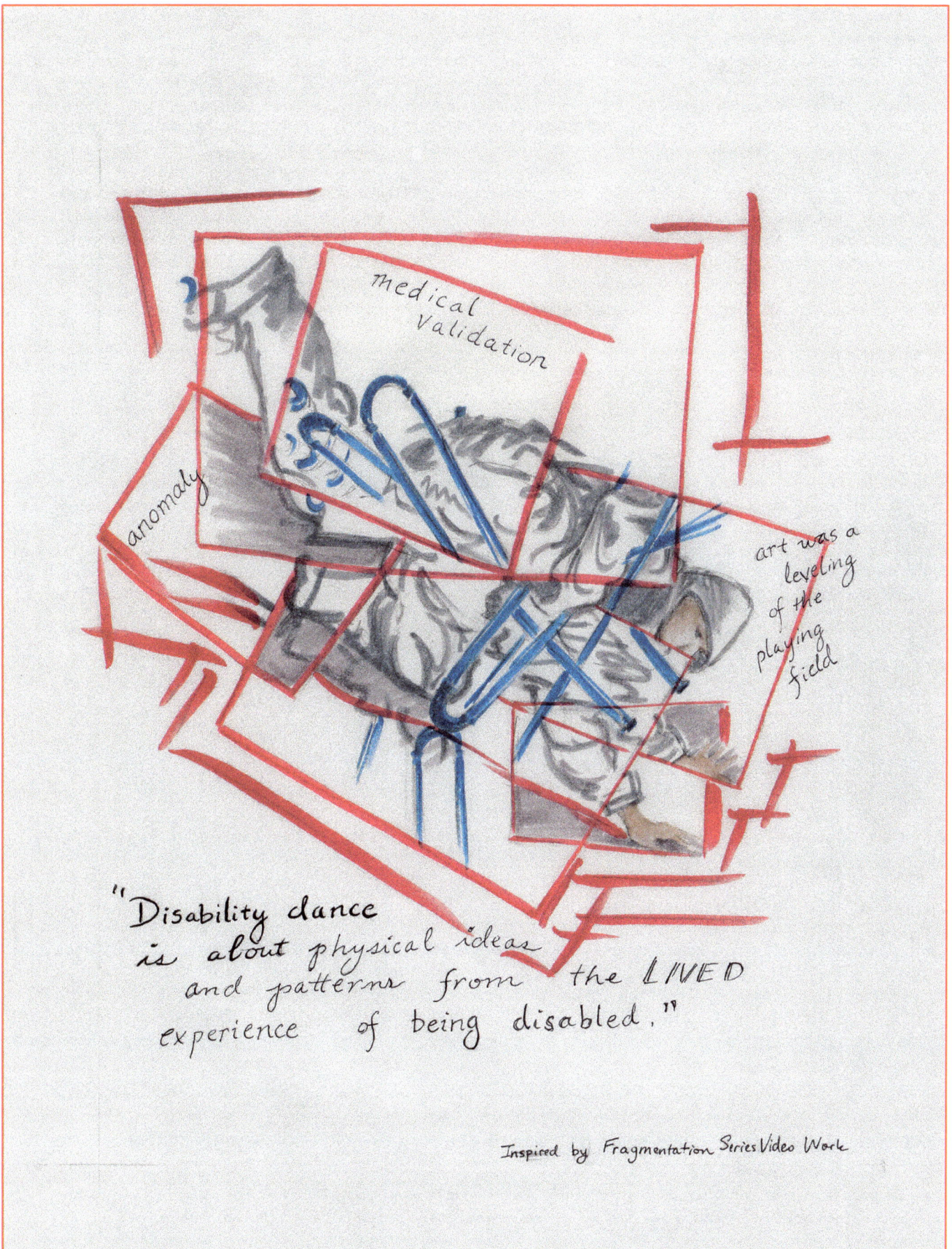

"Disability dance is about physical ideas and patterns from the LIVED experience of being disabled."

Inspired by Fragmentation Series Video Work

into the proscenium. While I was doing those group works, I was also touring a solo with a DJ called *Spatial Theory*, which went through the elements of my movement style on crutches, like a journey through the challenges of presenting the many aspects of my invented form. While doing the solo and group works, I was also performing a series of street performances called *Regarding the Fall* exploring sociological phenomenology in relation to complex representations of disability in public space. The street performances led into presenting recordings of those street works to a secondary audience in a video lecture format to frame the invented lexicon I had evolved to discuss and define the problematic nature of the phenomena addressed in that work. The feedback from the street series and the lecture series from academia, critics, and audiences fed into *Shannon Public Works Trilogy Window Bench Traffic*, which was a series of street performances focused on authenticity of audience experience viewing street-based work without disrupting the street. I also had a series of fabrications of different crutches to support the challenges of the evolution of my dance and video installations for dance contexts as a visual art practice. Through all the above projects, there was also an ongoing series of line art drawings based on my conceptual pursuits in my artmaking called *Notes on Performance*. That's the kind of interdisciplinary spectrum I continue to work within to this day as a dance practitioner.

When you tell people you are a dancer, what are the most common reactions you receive?

I don't tell people I am a dancer. When people ask what I do, I tell them that I'm a trans-disciplinary or interdisciplinary artist and my work revolves around questions and conceptual pursuits.

If I don't want to explain all that, I say I did choreography for Cirque du Soleil and I dance on crutches, which is a misrepresentation. Then they say, "Wow, really?"

What I did in dance was a technique 100 percent based in disability from childhood and based on the assumption of four points of weight distribution. It's not a translation of another form; it is based entirely in disability movement history and influenced by kinetic and stylistic elements of hip-hop and skate cultures. When I started dancing, disability dance was centered institutionally on wheelchair dance. If you were not using a chair or were able-bodied, you did not fit in very well. That was early on. In the past decade, I've experienced the shift of disabled dance into a broader spectrum of abilities and an alignment with queer theory and intersectionality. This transformation pushed the whole understanding of what a dancer is to the field of dance to a new place. Dance, to me, remains at its core the creative use of space, light, time, and the human condition.

> "Dance, to me, remains at its core the creative use of space, light, time, and the human condition.

What are some ways people discuss dance with regards to disability that you feel carry problematic implications or assumptions?

Because I was one of the earlier dancers with a disability to be covered by mainstream media, like the Village Voice and the New York Times, I was written about in ways I don't think would happen now. Writers and journalists have evolved to some extent. Because I'm not just a dancer and I also do visual art where my body is not a factor in the work, I've been able to experience writing about my work when my body is in it and when my body is not in it. The most problematic element in the former is the idea that the impetus for the creativity is the challenge of disability and not just an inherent desire to create. At the root of that is, "Nothing could stop them," or, "The condition drove them to…" That kind of language gives the credit for the impetus to be creative to a specific catalyst around disability. I find that especially true in dance because dance, even when it's not about disability, is couched in the challenge and landscape of the body.

The main thing I would say is to be careful of writing about the artist as a human-interest story. When I read articles about disabled artists, I often feel that they are trapped in a human-interest story, wherein the first three or four paragraphs are about the human-interest of disability and those details and, by the way, there's some art. That phenomenon needs to be looked at critically.

I invent language around my experience, and one of the terms I've come up with is "medical validation." Until you validate the nature of the disability in medical terms to an audience, they are not listening to what you are saying. They are wondering what the medical details are of the disability. I noticed how, in my live performances, I'd see people searching through their programs. Or their gaze would shift – they'd see I kind of use my legs and wonder if I really need crutches. I realized that if I do an introduction medically validating my disability and explaining my technique, then most people understand better how to appreciate my work. The ambiguous nature of my disability necessitates some form of validation of the use of crutches as an assistive device and not just a dramatic prop.

Do you believe there are adequate training opportunities for dancers with disabilities? If not, what areas would you specifically like to see improved?

Dancers with disabilities are few and far between. What needs to happen to make things better for disabled people to even believe that they can have a dance career is what needs to happen to make things better for everybody: Medicare for all, tuition free schools, student debt relief, military budget reduction, drawdown of the extraction energy model, etc. Without these core changes, dancers with disabilities will have difficult lives and less access to training.

Would you like to see disability in dance assimilated into the mainstream?

No.

What is your preferred term for the field?

Because my arts community is sometimes uneducated yet also genius, they might not know the "right way to talk" about things, yet are truly great people. I refuse to worry about terminology first or even second. Preferred terms come and go so I try not to get too attached to one or the other.

I don't think there's an absolute right way to talk about disability, though obviously there are some unacceptable terms that are derogatory.

In your perspective, is the field improving with time?

In the US, UK, Canada, Japan, Sweden, Germany, Finland, etc. – these Westernized, capitalist, or democratic-socialist systems – there are layers of support with different entry points for disabled dance makers. So yes, talking in this spectrum of humanity, the field is improving. In other parts of the world, however, the arts are diminished. All our advances in the US exist in a political bubble of human rights that ends at the tip of a warhead attached to a drone buzzing over the heads of poor people in other less accessible parts of the world.

Any other thoughts?

In one of my latest works, I taught able-bodied people the patterns and technique of my disability-based choreographed movements. If you're trying to learn a disabled form that is rooted in four points of distribution based on a crutch user, but you only have two points as legs without crutches, you're put in the same position as a disabled dancer translating a dance created for able bodies onto their own disabled selves. Thus, the work became a political statement about disabled dance in history as it relates to the able-bodied canon. I am arguing through the process of this work that you don't need a disabled body to perform a disabled dance. Disability dance is about physical ideas and patterns from the lived experience of being disabled. If others want to translate it to their able-bodied selves, it doesn't make it an able-bodied form; it simply modifies the original.

HANNA CORMICK

Hanna Cormick *is an Australian performance artist and curator with a background in physical theater, dance, circus, and interdisciplinary art. She is a graduate of Ecole Internationale de Théâtre Jacques Lecoq in Paris and Charles Sturt University's Acting degree in Australia. Hanna's practice has spanned many genres and continents over 20 years, including as a founding member of Australian interdisciplinary art-science group Last Man to Die, one half of Parisian cirque-cabaret duo Les Douleurs Exquises, and as a mask artist in France and Indonesia. Her current practice is a reclamation of body through radical visibility.*

"Not What My Body Does, But What My Body Is"
This interview was conducted by Emmaly Wiederholt in April 2020

How did you get into dance and what have been some highlights in your dance history?

My work exists as acts or embodiments. I don't always use the word "dance," as my work doesn't stay inside the conventional boundaries of what that label generally refers to. I did, however, have a fairly traditional dance formation: ballet, jazz, tap, contemporary, as well as belly dance and tango. Growing up with undiagnosed hypermobile Ehlers-Danlos Syndrome meant that I could do intensely flexible things with my body. This natural facility later led me to train as a circus contortionist. Back when I was young, it proved an asset.

My practice has always flowed across seemingly disparate styles, often pushing boundaries: butoh and Artaud, audience-interactive and site-specific experiments, or, with my company, Last Man to Die, exploring the interactions between the movements of my body and other artforms – computer percussion, interactive projected visuals – through the use of novel technology and artificial intelligence.

For a long time, mask was my obsession, both as a performer and as a mask-maker. I loved the total connection to the body and the intensity of the somatic trance-like experiences, as well as the physicality of carving wood and molding leather. A highlight was a year travelling between Bali and Australia apprenticing with the island's foremost mask-maker/dancer, Ida Bagus Anom. I continued with my mask practice by moving to Paris to study at Ecole Internationale de Théâtre Jacques Lecoq and apprenticed with Commedia master mask-maker Stefano Perocco di Meduna.

Mask was the impetus for training in Paris, but I slowly fell out of love with the form. I shifted towards forms influenced by my time with Ecole Lecoq, the Grotowski Center, and other experimental practitioners. I also trained in circus arts, delving into the underground cirque cabaret scene with my collaborator Apollo Garcia, specializing in La Danse Apache, where we mixed dance forms like tango and the Charleston with circus skills, including stage combat, acrobatics, and contortion. We spent time clowning with the Sirkhane Social Circus School on the Turkish-Syrian border with young Syrian and Yazidi refugees.

In 2015, my practice changed dramatically when I became disabled. I have a trifecta of genetic disorders: Ehlers-Danlos Syndrome, Mast Cell Activation Syndrome, and Postural Orthostatic Tachycardia Syndrome. These cause many secondary issues such as spinal instability, seizures, dystonia, and episodic paralysis. I'm a wheelchair-user now, and my immune system behaves as if it's allergic to everything: the odor of food, fragrance, chemicals, sunlight, and much more. I now live inside an air-sealed room. I can't be around most people and I can't go outside.

As a result of these restrictions, and the way in which my performance practice has evolved to accommodate them, my work now aligns more closely with live art or performance art. My coming out as a disabled performer was *The Mermaid*, performed over 2018 and remounted at the 2020 Sydney Festival. The piece was a physical representation of the social model of disability. In water, a mermaid can move freely, but on land she presents as disabled. Dressed as a mermaid, I was supported by my mobility aids and medical protective equipment: wheelchair, orthoses, splints, respirator mask, oxygen tank, and IV drip. Sharing the same physical space as the audience meant that I was exposed to the pollutants they brought into the space – chemicals, fragrance, bacteria – and that the performance could be interrupted at any point by allergic reactions, including anaphylaxis, seizures, or paralysis. The piece used my body as a microcosmic model of the environmental destruction we have wrought upon the planet through our actions. The fossil-fuels in an audience member's perfume would send my body into a dystonic storm or respiratory distress, just as the country was being assailed by bushfires triggered by fossil-fuel impacts on climate.

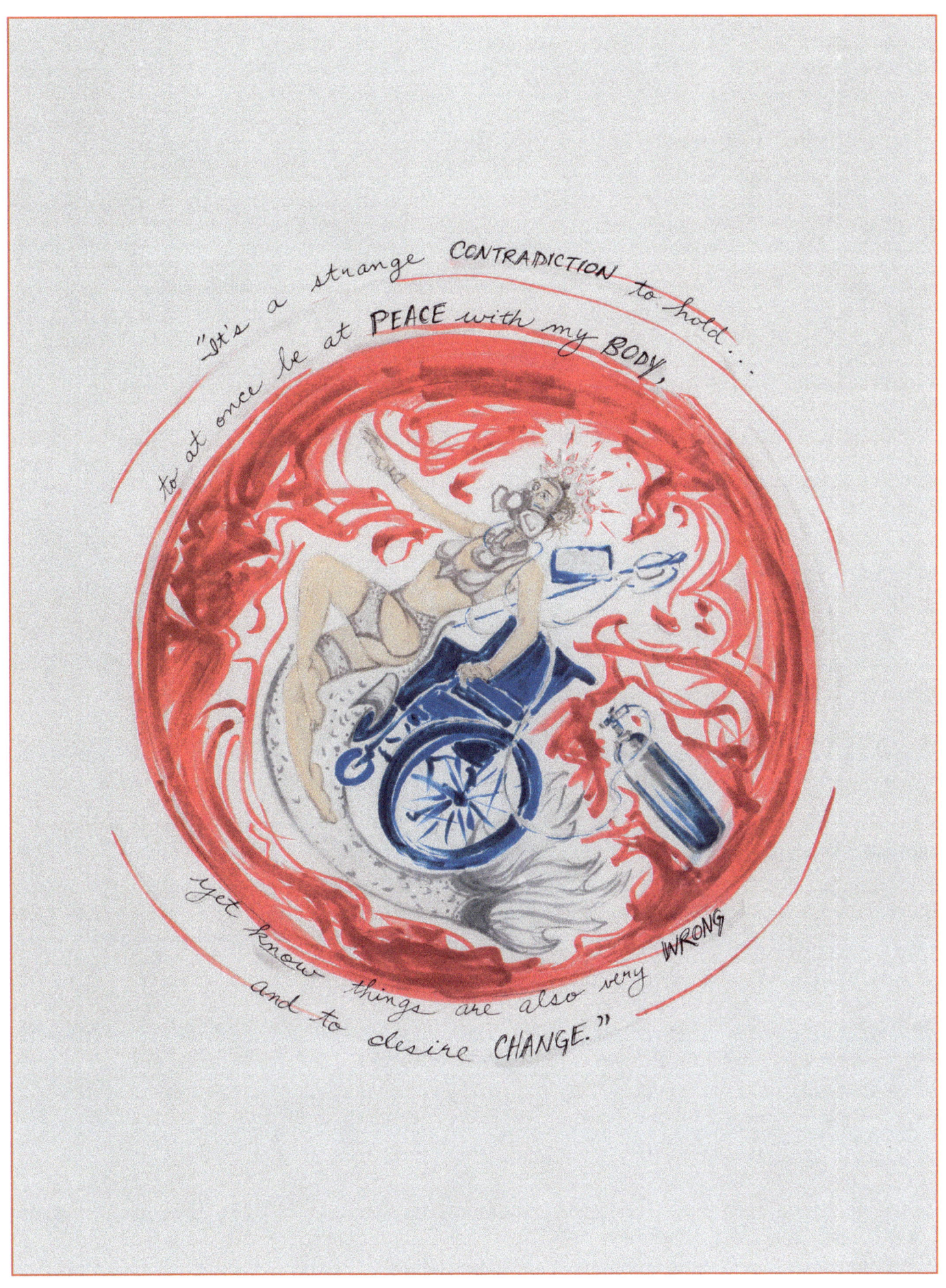

My performance works have been a practice in confronting shame and developing pride in disability, though I still encounter internalized ableism. Part of crip politics is to reject the notion of a cure, but when it comes to chronic illness, of course I would want to be cured. It's a strange contradiction to hold within myself; to at once be at peace with my body, yet know things are also very wrong and to desire change.

How would you describe your current dance practice?

It can be difficult to describe my practice to those who come from an arts culture in which "practice" is defined as productivity, repetition, and routine. I make space for Crip Time and non-extractivist modes of making: deceleration, pausing, irregularity, unreliability, and the radical levels of flexibility and responsiveness that are required to work with those values. Time doesn't exist in the same way when you are chronically ill; I don't have reliable day-to-day systems. I have limited amounts of energy, so I must be constantly aware of how much energy it takes for me to do something. Because it's highly destructive if I attempt to push through to get things done, I'm always measuring and monitoring. There are periods when I'm able to do more and other periods when I literally cannot move. My body calls the shots, not my will-force.

My work is no longer about what my body produces; it's not what my body does, but what my body is. My body's inabilities or lack of agency, its rebellious uncontrolled aspects, the conflict between a space and my body, all become choreographically relevant. It centers how I am moved by the space instead of how I move within it, as if I'm being danced by the environment and my body is a stage through which the dance passes.

It's a deeply disquieting sensation to let the moments in which I don't have control of my body – dystonia, seizures, paralysis – become public spectacle, but it's also empowering. These are the daily things that happen to me, and turning them into something that has artistic and political relevance reclaims these experiences from the dehumanized pathologized world of the medical, so they can come to mean more than the futility of invisible suffering.

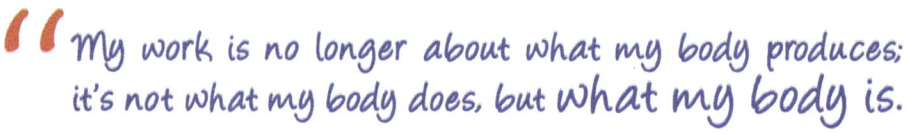

"My work is no longer about what my body produces; it's not what my body does, but what my body is."

When you tell people you are a dancer, what are the most common reactions you receive?

My immunological disability is the one people tend to focus on, rather than the physical barriers I face. For most people, the idea of living inside a bubble is so curious that they skip from, "She's in a wheelchair; how can she dance?" to, "She can't breathe normal air; how can she live?"

What are some ways people discuss dance with regards to disability that you feel carry problematic implications or assumptions?

The narrative of overcoming is really prevalent. On the one hand, there's a focus on the seeming insurmountability of my barriers with people using terms to describe me like "confined," "wheelchair bound," and "tragic." On the other hand, there's the use of words like "brave," "strong," and "fighter." I am uncomfortable with both, but particularly this language that glorifies strength and bravery. I am weak, my body is fragile, but are those necessarily bad things? Something I explore is the possibility of being fragile and still being a worthy artist, a worthy human.

Do you believe there are adequate training opportunities for dancers with disabilities? If not, what areas would you specifically like to see improved?

As someone who had professional training and a career before I became disabled, I'm aware of the privilege of having had that doorway into the industry. For people who either acquired their disability earlier in life or were born with a disability, it is much harder. I would like to see training programs that are accessible to disabled artists within institutions, and workshops that are accessible to people with atypical access requirements.

A lot of workshops are not accessible for someone with an immunological disability, and it's often considered outside the realm of access to have guidelines on the pollutants brought into a space – fragrance, makeup, food, drink – even though there may be strict guidelines on the types of footwear or clothing used.

I'm exploring how to transpose the Lecoq pedagogy for wheelchair-using bodies. The teachings of Lecoq are an integral part of my artistic psyche, but it now feels inaccessible to me since so much of the pedagogy is based around the idea of a neutral body. When you look at the body through this frame, any deviation from "neutral" becomes something that is being communicated. If you're using a mobility aid, your body is communicating disability. What if we instead viewed a wheelchair-using body, or other crip bodies, as their own forms of neutral? I want to reconcile my training with my new body, as well as make the pedagogy, which is a valuable creative framework, accessible for people who don't have a Lecoq-normative body.

Since the coronavirus, there has been an explosion of virtual dance spaces. On the one hand, it's great. This is access that people who are house-bound, bed-bound, or immunologically impaired have spent years fighting for. I'm excited by how the disability community has led innovation by drawing from pre-existing access tools, like creative audio description, to provide new ways of experiencing dance remotely. On the other hand, access to the virtual realm can be precarious for many disabled people, so it isn't a panacea.

Would you like to see disability in dance assimilated into the mainstream?

Disability performance should, as a genre, retain its own identity. When working in spaces that are specifically designed for disabled people and where everyone has an impairment, there's a certain freedom and ease of communication. But I believe mainstream dance should be accessible for disabled dancers as well, and disabled dancers, choreographers, and companies should be viewed as part of dance culture as a whole. I'd love to see dancers with disabilities get hired, not as a tokenistic gesture, but because we as artists bring something vibrant and unique.

What is your preferred term for the field?

I identify as "crip," which is a historic slur being politically reclaimed by a subset of the disability community. I would be comfortable with a non-disabled person referring to me that way, especially if they had checked about my preferred terms. But it is not an identifier one should externally place onto others without knowing if it is preferred, as some still receive it as an insult. If I was self-describing my work, I might refer to it as "crip performance," but if I was working with others, I might use a more widely used term like "disability dance."

In your perspective, is the field improving with time?

To me, it seems like a sudden bloom or renaissance but that might be because I've only been working as a disabled artist for a few years. When I first became disabled, I wasn't aware of the crip arts community. It has been exciting to discover subversive and bold performers creating works that are fascinating, moving, and politically provocative.

It feels like opportunities in the mainstream are improving. In the past year or two, there are more disabled performers in large arts festivals and more celebrities identifying as disabled or chronically ill, which reduces the stigma. I hope even more barriers will be removed as representation grows and culture shifts, so we can start to see true cultural equity.

LAUREL LAWSON

Laurel Lawson *joined Full Radius Dance in 2004 and has since performed extensively with the company as well as with other collaborations and solo projects, like Alice Sheppard's Kinetic Light. Career highlights include tours and a film appearance in HBO's* Warm Springs *in 2005. In addition to performing, choreographing, and teaching dance, Laurel is also an advocate, public speaker, para-ice hockey athlete, and the product designer and co-founder of an engineering consultancy based in Decatur, Georgia. Laurel was a 2019-2020 Dance/USA Artist Fellow.*

"We're Fighting for Artistic Acceptance"
This interview was conducted by Emmaly Wiederholt in May 2018

How did you get into dance and what have been some highlights in your dance history?

I came to dance almost by accident. My plan was to pursue an MD-PhD, but after running a lab as an undergrad, I burned out and took a gap year working as an actor and musician. I grew up in music and theater; I was onstage with a touring gospel band when I was four. One of my high school goals had been to go to a conservatory and double major in music and science. Unfortunately, my wrists did not agree; at one point I was practicing piano about six hours a day and blew out both wrists. Although I had to give up piano, it didn't sour me on music. I continued working on the side as a gigging musician through college.

A year after college, Douglas Scott, director of Full Radius Dance, taught a class at Shepherd Center, the premier Southeast rehab facility. It's a pretty big center for wheelchair users in Atlanta, and they host most of the sports teams, so I was in and out playing basketball and doing peer counseling. I figured, why not check out the dance class?

I was terrible. It was the first time I'd ever been exposed to modern dance. I'm not even sure I had seen a modern dance concert before. It was fun though, and interesting to be challenged as a complete beginner. A couple months later, Douglas sent me an email and asked me to audition for the company. I had no clue what I was getting into.

I was the only person auditioning that day. I took class with the company and then watched rehearsal. I still felt like I sucked, but I was asked to join the company. I thought, "Sure, I don't have anything going on in the mornings right now." Two months later, I was in my first performance in Kentucky. It was pretty overwhelming.

I'd been dancing just over two years when we did a national tour with Dancing Wheels and AXIS Dance Company. Evidently, dancing stuck. The first couple years are a bit of a blur; coming in as an adult and learning to be a professional dancer is a unique experience. I came to dance with a lifetime of athletic training and theatrical experience. Still, dance is completely different.

It's easy to remember tours as highlights. Italy was a big experience, but I'd also include among the highlights the experience working collaboratively in the company, like the first time a phrase I created made it into a final piece. There's also the first time I was recruited to work with a choreographer outside the company who didn't normally work in integrated dance. Finally, putting the piece *DESCENT* together with Alice Sheppard was a highlight.

How would you describe your current dance practice?

Like most dancers, it varies depending on the day. Right now, being in two companies (Kinetic Light with Alice Sheppard and Full Radius Dance) is really challenging. I dance six days a week. When Alice and I are touring or in a residency, we are basically doing 12 to 18-hour days, either in the studio or in active preparation or recovery. When I'm in Atlanta with Full Radius Dance, I might dance anywhere from three to five hours a day. I take class outside the company while on tour, as a lot of my favorite teachers are in New York or the Bay Area.

I also play para-ice hockey. If anything, I think dance informs hockey more than hockey informs dance. A hockey sled basically involves balancing on the blades of ice skates, but on your butt. It takes immense core strength. I lift weights regularly as well.

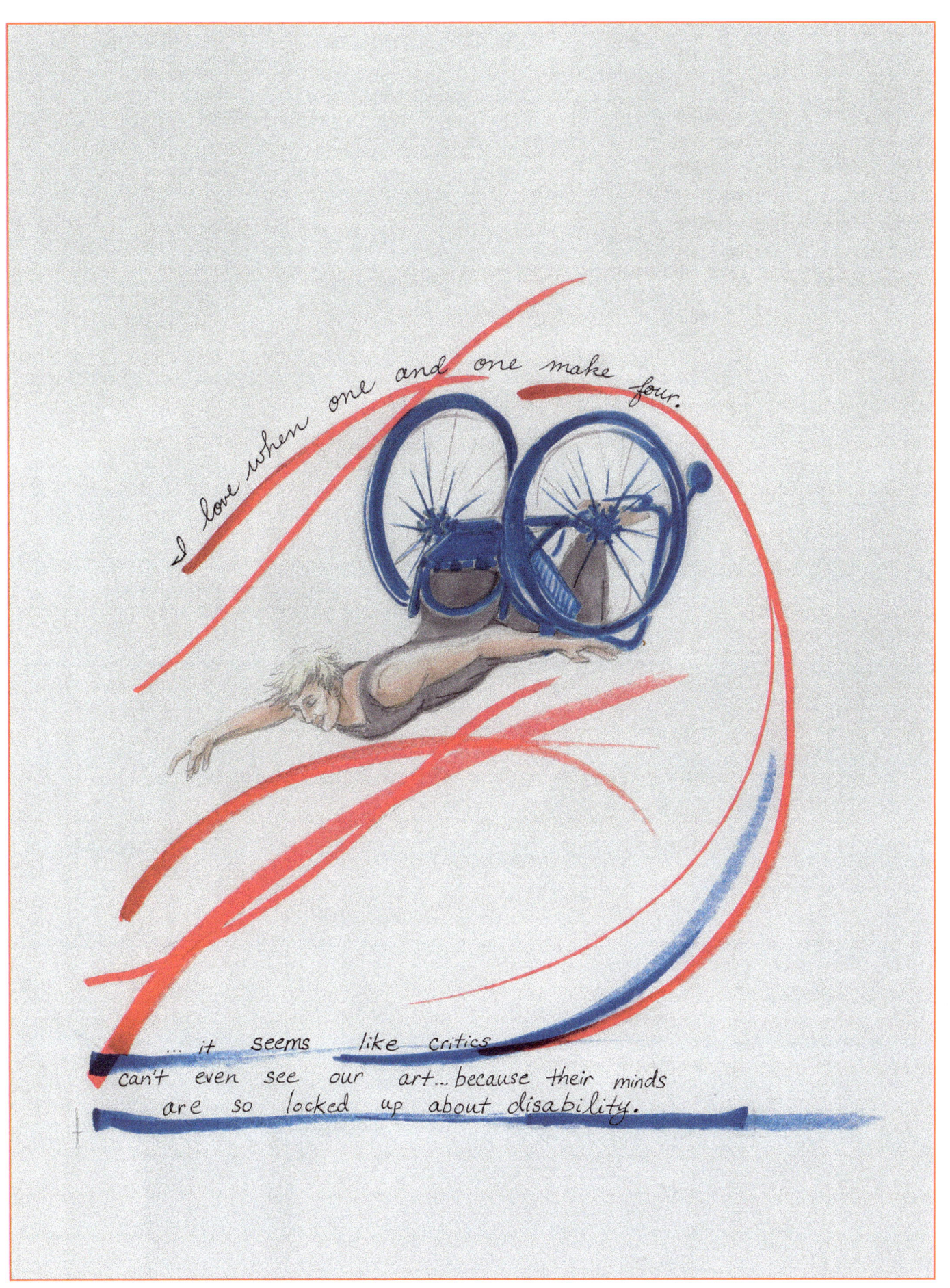

When you tell people you are a dancer, what are the most common reactions you receive?

When I started dancing, and for the better part of a decade, there was often either puzzlement or polite disbelief. I don't mind people being puzzled or confused; if they've never seen a disabled dancer, that's a legitimate reaction. I rarely get polite disbelief anymore. With people who are arts literate, there's a chance they may have seen some physically integrated dance. And now I can just show photos on my phone; "Show, don't tell," makes the conversation easier.

> "We were once fighting for legitimacy, to be allowed onstage at all. Now, we're fighting for artistic acceptance.

What are some ways people discuss dance with regards to disability that you feel carry problematic implications or assumptions?

The primary issue is that critics project their own narrative of disability onto what we do. Frequently, it seems like critics can't even see our art or technique because their minds are so locked up about disability. That's certainly not true of every writer. Some have done a good job educating themselves enough to write about what we're doing technically and artistically. It's about actually critiquing the work, instead of, "There are people in wheelchairs, and they don't move like I expected them to move." We want and need critics to think and write about our work, but it must move beyond the 101 level.

One review here in Atlanta particularly annoyed me because it referred to the disabled dancers as "performers" and the nondisabled dancers as "dancers." It was meant to be a good review, but the language choices made it clear what the critic implicitly thought. Every critic has biases, but in an ideal world, I see the job of the critic as coming from a clear place without projections or stating biases as artistic arbitration.

I find it extremely rare that people want to offend. Just knowing the terminology is helpful and understanding why "wheelchair bound" and "handicapped" are inappropriate and harmful. The overcoming and inspirational narrative is also something we're tired of. Dancers would like to be covered equitably. We've had instances where the dancers with disabilities are covered in depth to the exclusion of the nondisabled dancers, and that's not equitable either.

Do you believe there are adequate training opportunities for dancers with disabilities? If not, what areas would you specifically like to see improved?

Of course not. There are several key points in the training conversation. Not only is it difficult to learn as an adult, it creates a weird power dynamic. It's not uncommon for professional disabled dancers to have two or three years of experience and be dancing alongside nondisabled dancers with 15 or 20 years of experience.

That dynamic is something we try to be aware of in Full Radius Dance. That's why we've created an apprenticeship program. As we've brought in new dancers over the years, apprenticeship is one way to soften the entry to the art form. Apprentices usually take company class and understudy rehearsals, as well as do outside training.

Would I like more integrated classes for kids? Sure. Are we there yet? No. Teaching disabled kids is a whole other set of skills. Wheelchair technique is completely separate, and at this time I don't know anyone who isn't a full-time wheelchair user who can teach it. That means we have a serious shortage of teachers. Likewise with crutch technique. Teachers must also work with each individual's physicality in a way that is socially integrated and doesn't further 'other' the student. Disabled adults, especially those of us who have had our disabilities our entire lives, have a certain coping ability. It's problematic to subject a child to dance classes who might not necessarily have those coping skills yet. So it's not as easy as saying every dance studio should accept kids with disabilities because those teachers have to know what they're doing. Full Radius runs teacher trainings and accepts teaching students to try to get more people into the pipeline.

Would you like to see disability in dance assimilated into the mainstream?

I can see both sides of the question, and I come down on the side that disability dance should be assimilated into dance overall. However, there are people who will disagree with me, and point to my physical privilege that I can go into almost any dance class and take it if the teacher lets me. For a wheelchair-using dancer, a ballet barre is extremely advanced technique. There's not a one-to-one correlation of ballet technique to wheelchair technique. Another way to think about it is, if I go into a class that is taught to nondisabled dancers, I am doing three times as much mental work because I learn the original version of the choreography, I transpose it on the fly, and then I usually keep at least one variation of the transposition in my head. Being able to do that takes practice. Since disabled dancers have different bodies, it's not as easy as saying, "Activate this muscle."

I would love to see more disabled choreographers too. Marc Brew is doing an excellent job pioneering for us, with myself, Alice, and the handful of other disabled choreographers of our generation making work wherever we can. Disabled choreographers don't have to be restricted to working only with disabled dancers or physically integrated companies.

What is your preferred term for the field?

I prefer "disabled dancer." I am comfortable with "physically integrated," as it describes the dominant practice in the United States. "Disability dance," sure. I personally do not like "mixed ability." I feel it carries a power dynamic. With "mixed abilities," you can quickly think of the range of abilities represented, versus the fact everyone referred to is a professional dancer. It also stems from the etymology of dis-ability, which is antithetical to our current move toward disability as identity. "Inclusive dance" is gaining popularity, particularly for recreational programs. I think that works well, but also has problems, as it's not necessarily clear it includes disability. If you use "inclusive dance," you need to be clear about who you are including. One of the questions that comes with that term is whether inclusion extends to people with non-physical disabilities. This is something we facilitate at Full Radius in our classes and workshops. We have not, however, had a dancer with a non-physical disability audition for an apprenticeship or the professional company.

In your perspective, is the field improving with time?

I've been dancing for more than 14 years, and I've seen the field grow by leaps and bounds. There are a lot of contributors to that growth, like better communication and cross-pollination. As we've grown to have more experienced dancers in the field, we can push the boundaries of technique. That's a lot of what Alice and I are trying to do with Kinetic Light, by asking: What can disability do as a creative force?

We were once fighting for legitimacy, to be allowed onstage at all. Now, we're fighting for artistic acceptance.

Any other thoughts?

One question I've gotten recently is: Why should we have disabled dancers at all? Dance is about extraordinary physicality. As somatic researchers, disabled dancers have so many more options that haven't been explored yet. Nondisabled dancers must find it so hard to create, because any move in isolation has surely been done. With disability, we're still coming up with new moves all the time. It's quite exciting to be at this frontier of wide-open somatic research exploring dance in completely new ways. It's a key element of my practice. I've always been happiest in collaboration, improvising and riffing off what other people are doing. I love when one and one make four.

JERRON HERMAN

Jerron Herman *is a New York City-based interdisciplinary artist who employs dance, text, and visual storytelling. Originally from the Bay Area, he moved to New York City in 2009 to study Dramatic Writing at the Tisch School of the Arts at NYU. He then studied Media, Culture, and the Arts at The King's College, where he graduated in 2013. While in school, he began performing with Heidi Latsky Dance and quickly became a key member of the company. Jerron has performed at venues like Lincoln Center and The Whitney Museum of Art, and most recently is pursuing his own choreography.*

"A Political Understanding of Disability"

This interview was conducted by Silva Laukkanen in September 2018 and again in April 2020

How did you get into dance and what have been some highlights in your dance history?

Seán Curran, chair of the dance department at NYU, is who brought me into dance. I was an educational apprentice at The New Victory Theater in the summer of 2011, huffing the pavement trying to be a theater administrator and writer. That's why I came to New York. Seán was working at the theater then. On my first day he said, "I don't need an assistant. Why don't you just participate?" He was leading an intensive for public school teachers on how to integrate dance into their curriculum. It was the first time I was exposed to dance history and education. I guess Seán took a liking to me, because he encouraged me to make a solo that I showed for the final day of the workshop, which was also the last day of my internship.

All this time, Seán was telling me about a company in the city that created work with people with disabilities, Heidi Latsky Dance. One day, he literally handed me a ringing phone and it was Heidi's manager. I ended up in a studio the next week auditioning for Heidi. She said, "Show me what you got." It was a lot of improv over a two-hour session. At the end, she asked me my school schedule. Literally overnight, I became a professional dancer rehearsing with the company three to five times a week.

No one at school knew I was in a dance company. I didn't know how to tell people; it was just so different. I went to Boston for a gig on a Friday night, and my roommate and bestie started texting me, "Where are you? I haven't seen you in like 48 hours," and I was like, "I forgot to tell you, I'm performing in Boston right now, I'm a professional dancer."

One of my favorite memories was when we performed *GIMP* at Lincoln Center Out of Doors in 2012. I stepped in to replace Lawrence Carter-Long for his role in *GIMP*, and it was wild for me to be a replacement for a part that was specifically made for a person with cerebral palsy. At the time, I was the youngest member of the company. I really looked up to the other dancers, who were radical disability activists. And then the non-disabled cast members knew so much about the dance world. I was getting a mashup of disability history and dance education all at once, wrapped up in hardcore activism power.

How would you describe your current dance practice?

I'm interested in re-envisioning past events from my personal experience. The idea of memoir is so pervasive across disciplines, especially with respect to disability. I'm interested in abstracting and interrogating moments in my personal narrative, and then making them less personal so that people can insert themselves into them.

My most recent piece, *Phys, Ed*, is a solo that draws from my experience in PE as an adolescent, and then extracts and explodes it to transform the way we look at PE. That's my hope at least. The movement is focused on specific elements of the body, like balances, jumps, or pushups in gym class. I execute the movements differently because of my disability.

I had a residency in Staten Island for a month where I had studio time to just play and create. For a couple sessions, I explored how I could balance or use my gait in expressive ways. I went in cold one day and just worked out my trochanter and glute, and that became the choreography. There was this unintended effect of therapy or warming my body. I just moved how I move. In company settings, I interpret other people's choreography. This was a way for me to try out how I would move if I was the one asking.

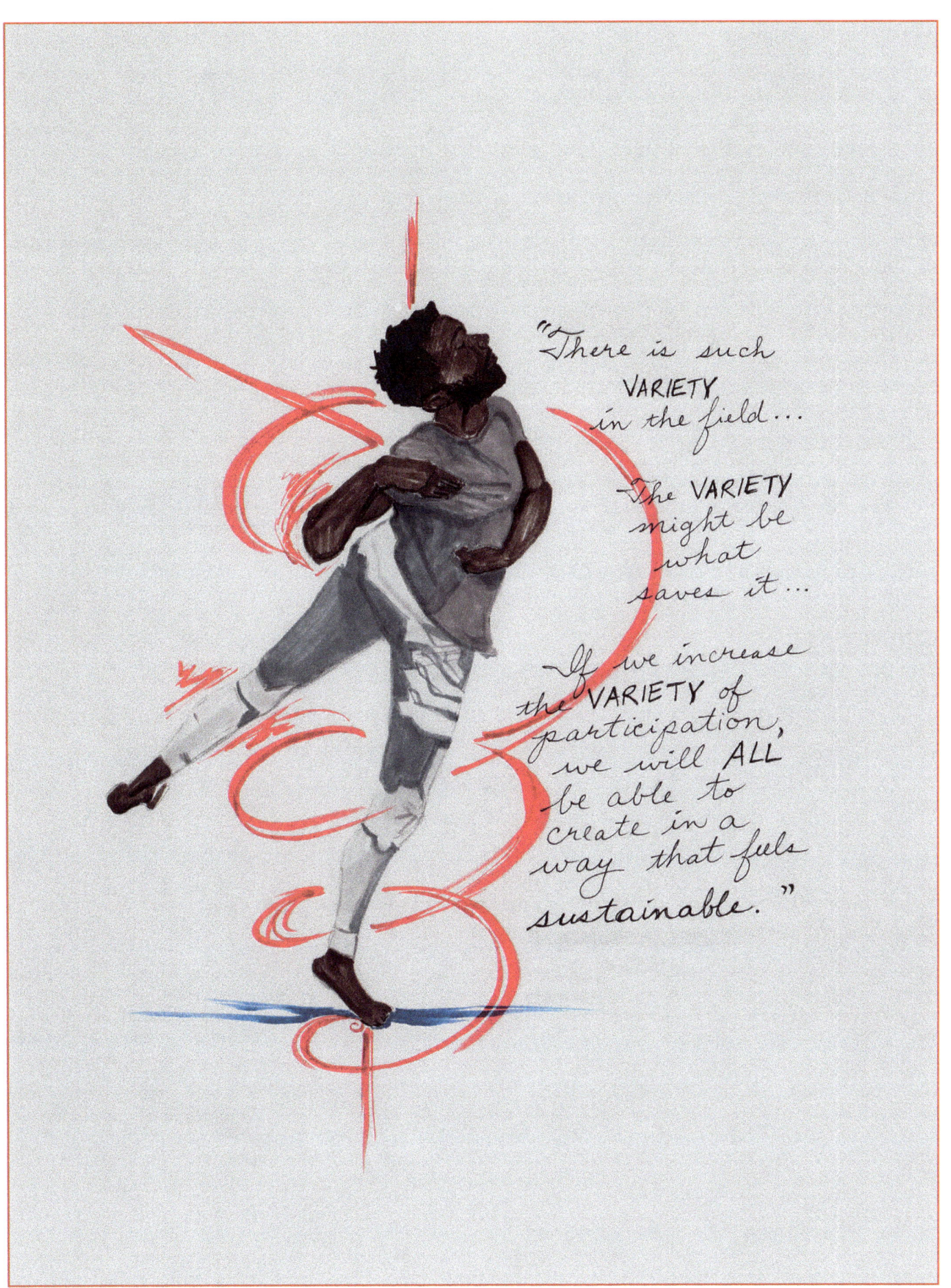

When you tell people you are a dancer, what are the most common reactions you receive?

Interest. Raised eyebrows. I think this is mostly because people don't see dance as a viable occupation. The first reaction is often, "You can support yourself?" It is always an economic question.

I know why people aren't as dubious with me as they would be with someone in a wheelchair or someone who is blind. I "present" as less disabled than others. That's definitely problematic. But the economic question irks me because people still don't give art its due. Being a professional is a novelty and considered kind of cute. People don't think, "Of course you work full time, of course you work as many hours as I do at my tech job." Art is placed on a lower social rung.

What are some ways people discuss dance with regards to disability that you feel carry problematic implications or assumptions?

There's no literacy. People are like: "I don't know what physically integrated or disability artistry means, so I am not going to learn. I don't know what it is, so I'm not going to engage." That reaction is in tandem with blatant ignorance and fear.

In a review of *GIMP* at Lincoln Center, the writer wrote that I gave the middle finger. At the time, my hand would spasm and break out in the middle finger. He thought it was my internal aggression toward able bodied people. Dude, I just had a spasm, and it manifested that way! Though I found it to be funny, the guy assumed he knew more about my disability than he did, and that was upsetting.

With regards to presenters and promoters, it's like there's this quota in the presenting schedule where there is only one slot for disability artists. It's this attitude of: "We presented AXIS Dance Company last year, so we don't need to present Heidi Latsky Dance this year." I am also curious about awards with respect to project grants that only pick one disability arts organization at a time. There is such variety in the field, and such variety is needed. I don't want the field reduced to a monolith. It would be such a shame if only one company or artist continues to get visibility, because different artists with disabilities offer different things. Pioneer Winter can satisfy something different than Alice Sheppard can. There is a need for many disabled dance artists to receive funding and opportunities, even within the same state or on the same side of the country.

> "I like "disability arts" as a framework because I recognize that the content, research, performance, and production elements all come from a political understanding of disability. When I hear "disability arts," I know it's going to be created for an audience who is disabled.

Do you believe there are adequate training opportunities for dancers with disabilities? If not, what areas would you specifically like to see improved?

Companies like AXIS have 30 years in terms of a foothold, so they get a lot of attention and they have their audience base. But the field is not creating new artists at the same rate as the non-disabled community. Artists from non-disabled dance companies become their own entities at a quick pace, but I don't see many individual artists coming out of companies like Full Radius, AXIS, or Heidi Latsky Dance and becoming their own entities. There is a real bottleneck in terms of what is possible. There aren't offshoots of collectives happening every year. There is just less on top of less.

Organizational support is key. It creates credibility in a real way. If we are asked to be on a panel, sit on a committee, or be on a board, it elevates that space, and it also elevates our voices. The networking that comes from that is crucial to change. Creating opportunities not only starts from leadership but also from dynamic participation. The solution is to take ground outside of the studio: to take ground in conferences, in educational settings, and in boardrooms at the same time as we are making work. We need more voices on the backend to inform what is being said and seen on the frontend. And there are more qualified people than I ever would have guessed; I am constantly being introduced to awesome artists who are ready to be in those rooms today.

The under 30 crowd is ready and available. I have a sense that the phenomenon of living under the ADA *[Americans with Disabilities Act]* has made younger people with disabilities more aware and qualified to disrupt places of power because we have been more integrated into society than previous generations. I never was placed in a special class, so I never thought my rights were separate. That helped my confidence; I've always thought I should be included.

Would you like to see disability in dance assimilated into the mainstream?

I fear disability in dance will go the way of every other category of dance. It will fight for the same kinds of toxic prestige and prominence as ballet, for example. It will become as exclusive as other forms. We will want the same awards and accolades. That is my only fear for disability in dance. I hope that, intrinsic to its nature, it can show other dance forms how different dance can be.

I am interested in how disability in dance doesn't go the way of codification. The variety of the field might be what saves it. I don't want disability in dance to become a monolith with a certain way of doing things that sells the tickets and gets the money.

What is your preferred term for the field?

I love "physically integrated" to talk about people with and without disabilities onstage together. It can also refer to the different ways that dancers with different disabilities, like an ambulatory dancer and a wheelchair dancer, might collaborate. Unfortunately, "physically integrated" is only talking about the physical expression of disability, not invisible, intellectual, or developmental disabilities.

I do not like "mixed abilities" because for me it doesn't refer to the body, it refers to mixing disciplines. I don't know about "inclusive" either. I think it's a buzzword that needs to be qualified because it is also used to refer to race and gender. There isn't a context of "inclusive" which just refers to disability, so it's unspecific.

I like "disability arts" as a framework because I recognize that the content, research, performance, and production elements all come from a political understanding of disability. When I hear "disability arts," I know it's going to be created for an audience who is disabled. "Disability arts" is disability specific.

In your perspective, is the field improving with time?

I said earlier that I fear the field will become a monolith. Our organizing needs to be deeper than just getting jobs in the dance world. We need to look at how disabled artists are working in other fields like theater, visual arts, and poetry. They have different perceptions on how to integrate aspects of accessibility that can be approached in dance as well. I love when disability arts are cross disciplinary and encompass a political identification so that our practices are under the same umbrella and we find solidarity. I feel optimistic and energized by that way of working together. If we increase the variety of participation, we will all be able to create in a way that feels sustainable.

ELIZABETH WINKELAAR

Elizabeth Winkelaar *is an artistic associate, company member, and teacher at Propeller Dance in Ottawa, Ontario. She earned a master's degree in Canadian Studies at Carleton University, which led to an interest in disability art and culture, as well as her involvement in Propeller Dance. She has taught outreach workshops, assisted with the children's program, and pioneered the company's seniors' program. She has further trained with Alito Alessi in DanceAbility, as well as with Persian dancer Maria Sabaye.*

"We're Blowing Disability Out of the Water"
This interview was conducted by Silva Laukkanen in May 2018

How did you get into dance and what have been some highlights in your dance history?

I was always interested in dance, but I was paralyzed in a motorcycle accident when I was 18. To me, that meant the end of dance. I became a schoolteacher instead. I got married and had two kids. I lived a normal life. But I got burnt out. Around that same time, I got divorced after 20 years of marriage. So my life kind of fell apart at 40 and I was faced with the realization that I was disabled and needed help. I came to Ottawa, met with an old professor of mine, and said, "I need to study and understand disability." I did my master's degree and started my PhD, studying the political economy around disability. I was trying to research how I could prove that disability was an asset to an economy, but I started to go a little crazy with it and I didn't feel like I had any allies.

Eleven years ago, I saw a poster on a wall advertising a dance class. It was of Shara Weaver, one of the co-directors of Propeller Dance, and it said, "Anyone can dance." I took the class and switched my whole life overnight. I had spent five years pursuing my degrees, but I decided very suddenly that dance was the answer I'd been seeking. I'd developed a political awareness of disability, but I didn't feel like I was actually going to make a difference by publishing papers and finishing my PhD. I had an opportunity to be a part of Propeller Dance instead, an awesome company that now has eight dancers in addition to community classes. And now I'm an artistic associate. I found my passion and creative voice.

The next big step was making a piece of choreography, which I didn't do until I'd been dancing for five years. The piece was called *Spasticus*, and it is now part of our company repertoire. It's always changing and evolving, and I'm still learning a lot from it.

The inspiration for *Spasticus* came from learning about the life of Ian Dury through the film *Sex & Drugs & Rock & Roll* and his song *Spasticus Autisticus*, which he wrote for the International Year of Disabled Persons in 1981. The BBC refused to play the song on the radio because they found it offensive. The song's reclaiming of language and rejection of the charity model struck a chord with each member of the company. We created the choreography by workshopping with the lyrics and with our own lived experiences of disability. In one sequence, one of the dancers is restrained in a straitjacket. The inspiration came from the dancer's own experience as a man with a cognitive disability.

How would you describe your current dance practice?

I'm a company member of Propeller Dance and an artistic associate. We have regular classes and rehearsals. I also teach in our outreach program. Outside of that, I've been studying Persian dance. My teacher, Maria Sabaye, is a remarkable woman and an expert on Persian culture. She offers me a whole new movement vocabulary. For example, the hand motions in Persian dance are very specific and meaningful. In Iran, Maria's home, the dances he practices and teaches are illegal. She's trying to rescue her dance traditions. I received a grant from the City of Ottawa's Creation and Production Fund to study with her. We've created some duets and done some small performances. So I have this other thing going on that feeds me in a different way.

Because of Propeller, the experience of collaboration has been essential to my understanding of dance. I like to work alone, or one-on-one, but I also like the opportunity to work with visual, musical, or installation artists. That's been very enriching. When I was in academia, I felt torn apart and isolated. I love what I do now, and I've never had any doubts about it.

When you tell people you are a dancer, what are the most common reactions you receive?

Confusion. A blank look. Not too many people go to the next step, but a few ask, "How do you do that?" That's the more curious response. And then there are even some people who say, "Great, tell me more." That's the most positive response.

What are some ways people discuss dance with regards to disability that you feel carry problematic implications or assumptions?

It's tricky with language sometimes. We keep saying again and again that it's not about therapy, it's about the art. Yes, of course, every one of our students – and right now we have more than 100 in our recreational and children's classes – say dance is important to their life and has a therapeutic aspect. But we try to stress the art of dance in our classes.

With regards to press, we love when we get a review that's done in the language of dance, instead of the language of inspiration or heroism. If the reviewer was surprised or entertained, that's great, but when they write about the movement itself and what they saw, that's wonderful. It's best to avoid words like "courageous," "inspirational," or "brave," but unfortunately these words are all too commonly used. I wish reviewers saw more – our strength, passion, and vulnerability. It's hard to get reviews in general. Now we're seeing more blogs about entertainment, arts, and culture. We're starting to get that feedback.

Do you believe there are adequate training opportunities for dancers with disabilities? If not, what areas would you specifically like to see improved?

No, of course not. It depends entirely on where you live, which is so unfair. Because Propeller is located in Ottawa, Canada's capital, there's a lot of money spent on the arts in a politically correct way. If you want to catch some Indigenous drumming, for example, come here, because this is where money is being spent on those kinds of artists. That's why I say it depends on where you live. I feel bad for people with disabilities who have no access whatsoever to movement, let alone dance. How are they going to find a dance class or yoga class? Whereas here, there are a lot of opportunities.

> "We're blowing disability out of the water. The new aesthetic asks the question: What does disability contribute to dance?

Would you like to see disability in dance assimilated into the mainstream?

Yes, absolutely. The time is right for that to happen, but you have to look at what that really means. For instance, more big dance companies are deciding they're going to have an accessible space of some sort, but what are they really offering? Are they offering tea for disabled girls with the ballerina? We don't want to get colonized. For more than 10 years, Propeller has offered contemporary dance classes for people of all ages and abilities. We have children, youth, and adult classes, always with a musician creating music for the class. We use inclusive exercises to explore space, time, balance, design, partner work, and musicality. Students have frequent performance opportunities. We have taught literally hundreds of students in the past decade. Many of these students have become beautifully skilled dancers.

There's a new aesthetic emerging. It's not just representing disability, but also, for example, obesity. It's saying we're beautiful. The new aesthetic goes beyond assumptions. It presents something the public doesn't expect, like the idea that disabled people have sex and romance. We're blowing disability out of the water. The new aesthetic asks the question: What does disability contribute to dance?

I've recently become more aware of the audience side. I'm trying to get more people of different disabilities into our audience. I've been networking with blind and Deaf people and finding out what they need to make that happen. Now we have a sign language interpreter.

I think we're a long way from becoming mainstream though. I live in a happy bubble of Propeller Dance. When I look at the movies people watch, the world is a long way behind. There's still a lot of inspiration porn. Look up Stella Young, who coined the term. We're in a bubble where we're pushing the boundaries of the arts world, but we don't know how to reach the greater public beyond our audiences and students. That's why I like the idea of digitizing our work and getting it out there. Propeller has strategic planning in the fall, and we need to find those new directions for our classes and company.

What is your preferred term for the field?

I like "integrated dance" but sometimes I also use "mixed abilities" to help people understand. Sometimes when I say, "integrated dance," people ask, "What are you integrating?" When I reply with the term, "mixed abilities," that gives them the answer. Coming from someone who is visibly physically disabled, they get it. Then sometimes they're curious about how that kind of dance works, and I like that curiosity. I think Indigenous and First Nations people also struggle with the same problem when it comes to terminology.

In your perspective, is the field improving with time?

Yes, we're gaining momentum. But it's very easy for us to fall into the trap of, "I've performed here and there," and thus think that everything is getting better. It's a much bigger project than that. Advocating for disability in dance has many dimensions. Increasingly, the big companies think they need to start integrating more. But I'd like to see them do it more mindfully and actually talk to us. Training and community outreach are important parts of the bigger picture.

EVAN RUGGIERO

Evan Ruggiero *is a singer, actor, one-legged tap dancer, and motivational speaker based in New York City. He began his professional tap career at the age of 10 with the New Jersey Tap Ensemble. He earned a BFA in Musical Theatre from Montclair State University. During college, he was diagnosed with osteosarcoma and had to amputate his leg to save his life in addition to undergoing multiple surgeries. Eighteen months after the amputation, and only two days after receiving his peg-leg, Evan was tapping again, this time in the vein of Clayton "Peg Leg" Bates.*

"Just Another Hustling Artist"
This interview was conducted by Emmaly Wiederholt in December 2018

How did you get into dance and what have been some highlights in your dance history?

I started dancing when I was five years old. I saw my sister in a dance class and thought it looked like fun. I started out in hip hop, which I really enjoyed, and from there started to take tap dance. By the age of 10, I had auditioned for a professional tap company, the New Jersey Tap Ensemble. I got in, and one of my first performances was at Lincoln Center. Some highlights throughout my career have included not only performing at Lincoln Center, but also at Carnegie Hall, on the Ellen DeGeneres Show, performing for Joe Biden, performing for President el-Sisi of Egypt, having my own show at the Kennedy Center, being a Drama Desk nominee in 2018… so many great moments.

When I was 19, I was diagnosed with osteosarcoma, a type of bone cancer. I had to leave school; I was studying musical theatre at Montclair State University. I started to undergo many treatments and surgeries. I always wanted to perform again and specifically to tap dance, but my cancer came back after seven months of surgeries and the only thing left to do was to amputate my right leg above the knee. I had heard of Peg Leg Bates, who was a tap dancer back in the day who lost his leg in a cotton gin accident when he was 12. He taught himself how to tap dance using a peg leg. I thought: If he could do it, so can I.

After the amputation, I went through 16 months of chemotherapy. Finally, after a total of two years' worth of treatments, I had a peg leg made for me and I began teaching myself how to tap dance again and get comfortable with this new extension of my body. From there, I started to perform again and travel the world not only doing tap dance but also singing, acting, and motivational speaking. I created something new for myself.

How would you describe your current dance practice?

I do a lot of rehearsing with my band, Evan and the S'Evan Legs – there are four of us, but only seven legs between us. As a tap dancer, I am also a musician, as many tap dancers will describe themselves. We rehearse maybe once a week together for four to eight hours. We are frequently booked for shows, so the amount of rehearsing we do is sometimes limited in comparison to the amount of performing we do. Depending on what show is coming up next, we'll get back into the studio to rehearse for it. New choreographic ideas are always being talked about and, when we have down time, we get into the studio to develop those ideas. From there, it's adding layers and building upon the foundation.

When you tell people you are a dancer, what are the most common reactions you receive?

Depending on which leg I'm wearing when I tell someone I'm a dancer, I might get a confused look. If it's obvious I'm wearing a prosthetic and you can see the robotics of my leg, some people will say, "What? You dance?" And when I say I'm a tap dancer, they are even more confused. I then explain to them that I tap dance with a peg leg. Then they might say, "Oh wow, crazy!" If I'm hiding my prosthetic under my pants leg, no one questions if I'm a dancer because they assume I have two legs. And then the real surprise is when I change into my peg leg and tap dance.

I still get the same looks and questions in a dance class. If I'm brought into a studio to teach, and it's advertised I have one leg, and my bio and photos are all available, the students might know what they are getting into. There's still the same reaction of: "What

happened to you?" I've created a new tap class for students who have two legs which replicates the sounds of what I'm doing with my peg leg. Students in my classes use their right heel to experience only having one way to make a sound out of their right foot.

What are some ways people discuss dance with regards to disability that you feel carry problematic implications or assumptions?

It happens all the time that I put my blood, sweat, and tears into a show and work on it for months, and the one thing that comes through in the press is something like: We commend him for what he's been through, and good for him. I don't want anyone to feel sorry for me. I'm just trying to present my work.

I get the inspirational thing daily. I'm flattered and am always grateful and appreciative to everyone who has reached out to me. At the end of the day though, I'm just another hustling artist trying to make a living and have a career. The odds are very much against all of us in this industry. On top of that, having one leg, I have to work three or four times as hard as someone with two legs. I don't look at my career as trying to be an inspiration to someone else. I have to get out there and just work harder.

I try not to see myself as disabled. I try to just keep going forward with where I left off when I had two legs. Every year, something on my list of goals gets checked off. There is a lot of negativity in the industry overall, but I think artists with disabilities are really starting to come out, make names for themselves, present their work, and say, "We are not ashamed of who we are." So I think the industry is starting to move in the right direction. Some disabled artists are even starting to get national recognition.

> *"I get the inspirational thing daily. I'm flattered and am always grateful and appreciative to everyone who has reached out to me. At the end of the day though, I'm just another hustling artist trying to make a living and have a career. The odds are very much against all of us in this industry.*

Do you believe there are adequate training opportunities for dancers with disabilities? If not, what areas would you specifically like to see improved?

There are companies like AXIS Dance Company and some others in New York that I've worked with that are dedicated to educating dancers with disabilities. In the more commercial world, I haven't seen those educational opportunities. I've reached out to a couple other amputees who are interested in learning tap dancing, but there's no institutional training opportunities at the moment. It's individuals coming together to educate each other, and then maybe a company gets behind it.

I was in college when I had my leg amputated. I was a musical theatre major, so I was able to focus on singing and acting after my surgeries. By the time I had lost my leg, my university was willing to work with me so that I had the right credits for my dance classes. As a freshman, I had taken four days of ballet, two days of jazz, and two days of tap, so I had fulfilled most of my dancing requirements. As I taught myself how to dance with a peg leg, I took double tap classes to make up the final credits. My amputation didn't put much of a hold on my college academics, but it's interesting to speculate if my experience would have been different if I'd had my amputation before college.

I taught myself how to dance with a peg leg by studying the footage of Peg Leg Bates. Knowing it could be done, I tried to recreate what he did and then make it my own. Tap dancers think of themselves as musicians, so I tried to think of it as creating new music with this extension of my body. I used the peg leg as the bass drum, and I used my left foot as the snare and tom-tom drum. Through the sounds I was able to create, I came up with a new technique for myself.

Would you like to see disability in dance assimilated into the mainstream?

I think that dancers with disabilities should very much be integrated into the mainstream, as I have been trying to do for the past eight years. I have been a little successful with it. The best way to go about getting disability accepted in dance is to integrate it into the commercial world. It's on its way, but it's going to continue to be a struggle finding producers interested in working with dancers with disabilities and seeing us as commercially profitable.

What is your preferred term for the field?

Sometimes the press will call me "differently abled." The correct way to say it is to call it a disability. I call myself a one-legged tap dancer or a one-legged song-and-dance man. I prefer "dancer/actor/performer with a disability" or "dancer with one leg."

In your perspective, is the field improving with time?

I believe it is. We're seeing more commercial work featuring dancers with disabilities. It is still about having that discussion with casting directors and other producers who are willing to take a dive into this work. We don't want to be a gimmick in any way. We are hardworking performers and casting us can be profitable.

NASTIJA FIJOLIČ

Nastija Fijolič *is a Slovenian photographer, vlogger, and competitive ballroom dancer who competes in World Para Dance Sport. She was born with spinal muscular dystrophy and uses a wheelchair.*

"Judge Me as A Dancer, Not as A Wheelchair Dancer"
This interview was conducted by Silva Laukkanen in February 2021

How did you get into dance and what have been some highlights in your dance history?

When I was young, I thought dance was so girly. I studied photography and filmmaking, and I ended up making a promo video for a para dance club. I said, "Man, that looks fun, I bet with a trainer I could dance a little bit." I tried it and stayed and started to compete. It's been eight years now. I was hooked immediately by the music, the movement, the energy of the competition, the drive. And the people became like family. When I go to competitions, I know almost everybody even though it's like 150 dancers.

I dance ballroom, mostly Latin. I have a walking dance partner. We call this *combi* because it combines one person in a wheelchair and one standing dancer. We also have *single*, which is a dancer on their own, and *duo*, which is two dancers in wheelchairs. There are three basic categories, which includes Latin and freestyle. And in all that, we have class one and class two. Class one is people who are more disabled, like they have a spinal injury. Class two is people without an arm or leg. I am class one because I use an electric wheelchair in everyday life, but I use a manual wheelchair when I dance. That's a rough description of para dance sport.

A highlight was placing second in the European Championship two or three years ago with my wheelchair dance partner, so in *duo*. That was quite surprising because we didn't expect it. There were a lot of people competing in the Latin and freestyle category, and we took second place.

If I'm honest, competition is really hard for me because there are people with different kinds of disabilities in the competition. I have spinal muscular dystrophy, which means my muscles are not strong enough to push myself really fast or do the same move 10 times equally. I can do it maybe three times, but I compete with people who don't have that kind of disability. They might have a spine injury from the waist down, but they have normal hands. I go, do my best, and see what happens. That's why second place was surprising, because I didn't expect it.

How would you describe your current dance practice?

Before the pandemic, we had group lessons two times per week for everyone in the dance club. It was to improve the movement and to physically get stronger and more prepared. When I dance, I mostly use my upper body, so I have to get physiotherapy one or two times a week for my legs and my spine. And then, from time to time, my partner and I work with a trainer to improve the choreography and make some movements better. Being physical four to five times a week is the maximum for me. I cannot do more because my muscles need time to rest. Two or three days before a competition, I do not train. It took me like three years to figure that out. We used to train extra before a competition and then I wouldn't be able to move my arms. I decided maybe I needed to rest beforehand, and it was better.

When you tell people you are a dancer, what are the most common reactions you receive?

People still don't accept para dancing as a sport. Have you seen the dancers in our competition? They're really good. They do stuff that dancers in standing competitions do. I think people will eventually start to see it as a sport, but there's not that mindset yet. When people see a dancer in an electric wheelchair, they're like, "Oh, he or she is dancing, let's clap." Can I just punch those people

in the face? That dancer in the wheelchair dances as much as he or she can. You have to be an artist to understand that. It's the same with judges in competitions. They put me in fifth place because I'm not fast. I feel the music just as much as the person in third place. Para sport will never be fair because it's not two people competing with the same injury or disability. But for the people who think para dance is not even a sport, I hope they figure it out.

What are some ways people discuss dance with regards to disability that you feel carry problematic implications or assumptions?

When people say, "You're so inspirational," I'm like, "Really? I feel sorry for you if I am an inspiration for you." When I started dancing, I felt like everybody clapped for me because I'm in a wheelchair. I wondered: Did they see my dancing, or did they just see my wheelchair? That's why I love to compete in para dance even though I know I will not win because I know they will judge me as a dancer, not as a wheelchair dancer.

The biggest "come on" moment is when I see the title of an article like, "She's in a wheelchair, but she's still dancing." Maybe they could write, "She's dancing, and she's in a wheelchair," or just, "She's dancing." I work in media, so I know the title has to be something that people will click and read. I get it. But see the person, not the thing they move with.

Another problem is we have these competitions all over the world, but we travel to a hotel that has two rooms that are accessible, and we have 100 people in wheelchairs. In the bathtub or shower there is a step. I'm like, "Shit, what now?" Some people in wheelchairs can move themselves with their arms, but I can't. We somehow manage. Paula is one of the dancers who always gets the accessible room. I ask her if I can shower in her room because the shower is accessible. That's what I love about our competitions: We can help each other and still be competitive.

In Slovenia we don't have funding, and my dance wheelchair is the first thing I need to dance. I can still dance without my fake eyelashes, but I cannot dance without my wheels. In the Netherlands, if you compete in a sport for the country, you get new equipment every three years, like a new wheelchair or new skateboard. I bought my manual wheelchair and that's it for life. And it was not cheap.

Those are some of the biggest problems in para dance sport, but mostly, I would really love to see all the people clap for me because of my dancing, not because of my disability.

> "I love to compete in para dance even though I know I will not win because I know they will judge me as a dancer, not as a wheelchair dancer."

Do you believe there are adequate training opportunities for dancers with disabilities? If not, what areas would you specifically like to see improved?

No, of course not. In my country we have one dance club that teaches para dance sport. Some people would say dance is dance so every club should teach para dance sport, but there are specific things that standing dancers don't understand, like how to turn your wheelchair or how to use your body to make a roll. I live close enough to the club in Ljubljana that it's not a problem, but for people who live two hours from here, they will not drive that far every other day to train.

The other thing is studios are not accessible. Where we train is only half accessible; I cannot go to the toilet, for example, because it's too small. In Slovenia I haven't found any studio that is totally accessible. This is another reason why we cannot train everywhere.

For three or four years now, para dance has been included in national competitions, but in January there was a competition and we were not invited. Our trainer said, "What's the problem? We are part of your dancing community and a national sport. Why were we not included?" They said, "In the rules it's written that only athletes can dance." Our trainer was like, "Are you joking? They're para athletes, so therefore they can compete." They still don't include us. We always have to push them. We always have to say, "Is this dance hall accessible? Are there toilets for wheelchair users? Where will we have room to get dressed?"

Would you like to see disability in dance assimilated into the mainstream?

We would love to be included. We would love for standing people to know we exist and dance the same and train. This is getting better every year because from time to time, our coach and the standing coach meet, and they make one big training with all the standing dancers and para dancers together. We all dance to the same music on the same floor at the same time.

But I still think it has to be separated because we are rolling, and they are walking. These are two very different things. I would prefer to separate into disabilities even further because if I know a dancer's disability, I can tell a lot about how they will move best. If I see a person with cerebral palsy, I know they cannot make gentle moves. They will have spasms, so I cannot expect them to be really smooth. That's why I think it's important to know what disabilities people have.

Like I said earlier, in competitions we have class one and class two. Before every competition, there are four or five judges who ask us to put our hands in the air or do rotations, and they give us points. In the end, how many points you get determines which class you get put into. They put me in class two three times because I can put my arms up, but I cannot do it fast. They are like, "Can you do it, or can't you?" If I say I cannot do it, and they see me do it on the dance floor, I will be suspended. Eventually, they understood and put me in class one.

What is your preferred term for the field?

Five years ago it was still "wheelchair dance sport," but now it's "para dance sport." I think "para" is the best word. It sounds more professional. I would like to avoid "disability," "handicapped," or "wheelchair" to describe our dance.

It would be awesome if there was just "ballroom dancing," but para dance is different than walking so it must be called something else. We did this project with Toyota a few years ago and they had this quote: "Make your disability ability." I was like, yeah! Though I generally avoid words like "disability" because it has the association of pity.

In your perspective, is the field improving with time?

Of course it is. If it's not getting better, then why are we doing it? Every year more people are included. More people know about our club or para dancing in general. Slowly we are getting there. With the coronavirus, I think it went five steps back, but it will get better. It has to.

ALEXANDRIA WAILES

Alexandria Wailes *has worked as an actor, director, choreographer, and American Sign Language (ASL) consultant in television, film, music videos, web series, Broadway, and Off Broadway. She toured with the Deaf West Broadway production of* Big River, *served as the associate choreographer for the Tony-nominated Deaf West production of* Spring Awakening, *was a member of the Heidi Latsky Dance Company, worked as a museum educator for the Whitney Museum of American Art, and was a teaching artist with Theatre Development Fund and Interactive Drama for Education and Awareness in the Schools, Inc.*

"Let us move!"

This interview was conducted by Emmaly Wiederholt in June 2019

How did you get into dance and what have been some highlights in your dance history?

My first exposure to dance was when I was two or three years old. After I contracted and recovered from meningitis at 13 months old, doctors gave my parents several suggestions. One doctor suggested I be placed in dance classes. He said, "It will be good for her balance and physical coordination." All around the same time I learned dance, sign language, and obtained speech and auditory hearing training for what I had to work with. I think of the vocabulary of dance as my foundation in communication. My parents told me that once I was introduced to dance classes, that was it, I was taken with it.

For much of my childhood and early teen years, with a few gap years, I went to dance classes on weekends and after school. As a teenager, I decided to reimmerse myself. I had become more conscientious of how I sounded when I was speaking. When I got back into dance, it was very cathartic and freeing. However, I didn't have the classical ballet body even though I was classically trained. It was an ongoing journey of trying to understand where I fit.

For college, I attended The University of the Arts in Philadelphia where I was the only Deaf person in the dance department. It was definitely a very interesting and fantastic experience, yet a challenging journey because there was a real culture shock in communication the first year. Let's back up a bit. While I was in my second year of high school, one of my teachers at Delaware School for the Deaf informed me and my parents about this summer intensive performing arts program at Gallaudet University. It was called the Young Scholars Program and it brought in high schoolers from all over the country. The month-long intensive had a faculty that was predominantly Deaf; this is where I met my first ever professional Deaf dance instructors. I ended up transferring over to the Model Secondary School for the Deaf (MSSD), which is on Gallaudet's campus, for the last two years of high school. Returning to a predominantly hearing environment for college was challenging, as ASL was not the common language used among my peers and teachers.

During those years, there were many highlights. Thanks to the strong performing arts program at MSSD, I performed in Senegal. During and after college, I performed with a group from Washington, D.C. in Japan, India, and Romania.

I got into choreography after college. It's difficult auditioning and going to dance classes when you don't have money and are barely paying the rent, even with roommates. That's when I started venturing into acting, directing, and choreographing. In 2002, I choreographed for and performed with a collective of dancers in Washington, D.C. called Pentimento for Deaf Way II International Arts Festival. It was called Pentimento based on the idea of an oil painting, how new layers can be added and then stripped off to reveal the backstory of the canvas. It was a short-lived company as the members were from around the country and world.

Over the course of 20 years, my work as a teaching artist, choreographer, actor, dancer, and director has enriched my journey as an artist. I taught workshops on contemporary dance and hip hop with high school students. I worked with the Heidi Latsky Dance company for a few years and ended up performing at American Dance Festival in my late 30s, which goes to show it is never too late! I worked as the associate choreographer on the Deaf West production Broadway revival of *Spring Awakening*. My latest collaboration as a choreographer was with Spellbound Theatre which focuses on immersive theater for babies, toddlers, and their guardians.

How would you describe your current dance practice?

Full disclosure: I'm not dancing as much as I used to. I haven't been able to afford taking dance classes, and much of my schedule has been focused on artistic sign language consulting and directing for the stage, TV, and film. Unfortunately, that means a lot of time sitting on the creative's side of the table working with my colleagues and with the actors. Despite not actively dancing as much, my inherent sensibility of movement has informed many of my choices made in productions that incorporate ASL. A lot of the work I do with the actors is watching and supporting them in how to be, move, and use space while signing.

I work as the director of artistic sign language. The job used to be called an ASL consultant or a sign master. It's a combination of choreography and dialect coaching. It's often confused with interpreting, which it is not. An interpreter facilitates communication between a non-ASL user and an ASL user. A director of artistic sign language is completely focused on the authenticity of the storytelling, the sign choices made by the director, actors, and other members of the creative team, basically how language lives in and on the body. For example, if you have one Deaf character in a piece and everyone else is hearing, how do they interact? I explore those possibilities. Because sign language is very physical and spatial, my work in artistic sign language is informed by my dance history.

Back to my dance practice, I'm about to enter a new phase. I am currently an actor/dancer in The Public Theater's *For Colored Girls Who Have Considered Suicide/When the Rainbow is Enuf*. It's nice to be dancing a lot and telling stories through movement, gestures, and ASL.

When you tell people you are a dancer, what are the most common reactions you receive?

"Really?" That's one. If they are hearing, they always say, "How can you hear the music?" If they're Deaf, they say, "You can't be a dancer." It's just part of our history, this idea that music lives in the senses of the hearing. However, that's not true; music and sound function on all levels through the vibrations. Musicality and rhythm are in our bodies. But if people think dance is tied to music and music is something you hear, then it doesn't compute that I'm a dancer.

What are some ways people discuss dance with regards to disability that you feel carry problematic implications or assumptions?

> "We don't have time for this inspiration narrative anymore. Let us move! We have a lot to clear so we can do our thing.

The common phrase that comes up is one of inspiration or pity, like, "How are you doing that?" said with surprise. It comes across as sympathetic, but when you're on the receiving end, it feels icky. When you get that more often than not, you start to question what you are doing to begin with. That kind of reaction isn't about how I've manipulated or expanded the vocabulary of dance. It's more like, "Oh wow, good for you, you're so beautiful." It's very stereotypical, instead of letting my work challenge people or engage in critical thinking and conversations about how dance lives within the body.

I've always believed that dance is equal parts musicality, technique, and soul. How can you communicate the soul and bring it forth into space? A lot of Western classically trained dance is strongly focused on technique. For dancers with disabilities, the bar is Western dance technique. That's the expectation we must hit. So when we dance, the reaction is often, "Ah! Wow! Good for you! That's amazing! So beautiful!" I read it as ingenuine. They just see the physicality of the body and are not thinking about how the person dancing is expressing themselves. We're just inspiration for them. I think that's our biggest barrier. But we don't have time for this inspiration narrative anymore. Let us move! We have a lot to clear so we can do our thing.

Do you believe there are adequate training opportunities for dancers with disabilities? If not, what areas would you specifically like to see improved?

There's a huge lack of easily accessible studios. I'm talking on an architectural level. Some dance studios are walkup, or there's one elevator that people in wheelchairs can ride with the trash. It's ridiculous. Of course, in an older city like New York City, things cost a lot of money to renovate, but we need to find creative solutions.

I also think dancers with disabilities need more exposure to different types of dance across the board. We need more dance teachers who are working with low vision dancers, or people in wheelchairs, or those with a missing limb. Dance is often segregated.

Dance is how you live and move in your body. How you move in space, that to me is dance. I want to challenge perceptions of how bodies can move in space.

Would you like to see disability in dance assimilated into the mainstream?

Yes and no. If you have different bodies in space, that's fantastic; the experience of interactions, exposure, experimentation, and play helps people to better understand each other just by the diversity in the room. But some spaces are better suited for common ground and expressing communication. When I dance with a company of all-hearing people, for example, there's always going to be the process of deciding to bring in an interpreter. Communication is faster with an all-Deaf company, and there's none of that "What can you hear?" or "Let's use sign language as part of the choreography because it's so beautiful" sentiment. This is my language! There's definitely merit in having spaces where we can come together, feel safe, and create. That's equally important. Most able-bodied hearing dance companies have never worked with a Deaf person. But we're always the minority accommodating the majority, instead of everyone working together.

What is your preferred term for the field?

Speaking for myself, not for my community, it depends on who I'm interacting with. I give myself permission to say, "I'm a Deaf dancer," or, "I'm a dancer who happens to be Deaf." I use those interchangeably.

A company might say it has a range of dancers with different abilities but, to me, that description sounds like a hot soundbite. I just want it to be a dance company, nothing attached to it. A descriptor like that might be in the company's mission, but I like to stay away from the pity or the inspiration porn complex. I want to avoid that language.

In your perspective, is the field improving with time?

Slowly but surely. There's definitely more awareness out there and more visibility and opportunities. As far as shifting society's frame, one person can't do all that work; it takes a vast community with everyone being a part.

Any other thoughts?

It's important for dance companies to have in their line budget funding to allow for dancers with disabilities to be a part of the conversation. Have an interpreter in the audience or auditory descriptions for people with low or no vision. Rent spaces that are accessible. It goes back to education.

MARC BREW

"I Claim It: I Am A Disabled Man"

This interview was conducted by Emmaly Wiederholt in May 2018

Marc Brew *has worked for more than 20 years as a director, choreographer, dancer, and teacher with the Australian Ballet, PACT Ballet, Infinity Dance Theater, Candoco Dance Company, and AXIS Dance Company. Marc was associate director of Scottish Dance Theatre and Ballet Cymru, and associate artist at Tramway Theatre. Since 2008, Marc has focused on his own choreography with Marc Brew Company. Other choreographic commissions include Scottish Ballet, YDance, Touch Compass, Amy Seiwert's Imagery, GDance Academy, Greenwich+Docklands International Festival, and City of London Festival. Marc was also artistic director of AXIS Dance Company in Oakland, California.*

How did you get into dance and what have been some highlights in your dance history?

I grew up in a rural village called Jerilderie in Australia with a population of 900. Growing up, it was just my mother and myself. My mother's best friend's daughter was my same age, and we were good friends. She started taking a jazz dance class and I joined. A teacher would tour to different country towns and came through Jerilderie on Fridays. Being the only boy, I was teased a lot, so I quit. My teacher and the other girls encouraged me to keep going, so I went back. I began making dance routines at lunchtime with the girls in the schoolyard, and my schoolteacher asked me to perform at morning assemblies.

When it was time to look at high schools, my mother, schoolteacher, and dance teacher decided it was better for me to apply to arts schools in Melbourne and Sydney than to go to the local high school 30 kilometers away. I auditioned and was accepted with scholarships to both schools. I ended up choosing the school in Melbourne, as it was a bit closer to my hometown (a four-hour drive).

It was a huge shift to move away from home at age 11. I was homesick, but I finally felt like I fit in. There were two other boys in my year. I studied ballet, contemporary dance, jazz, character dance, anatomy, and academic studies. My interest in choreography was also nurtured; I was given opportunities to choreograph on other students.

Once I graduated, I studied for another three years at the Australian Ballet School where I also danced with the Australian Ballet. From there, I was offered a job with PACT Ballet in South Africa, where I met many great people and danced many great ballets.

One Saturday afternoon, three friends and I went for a drive to a game reserve just out of Johannesburg. We were on the highway when a drunk driver drove down the wrong side of the road and hit our car head on at high speed. My three friends were killed, and I survived with massive internal injuries. A week later, I woke up with my mum and aunty at my side, and a doctor told me I was paralyzed from the neck down. Once I got back to Australia and went through rehabilitation, I learned about my spinal cord injury and what it meant. I started getting mobility back, and was able to move my fingers and arms, but it stopped at my chest.

Many of my dance friends couldn't bear to see me; I was their worst fear. I spent six months in rehab and then tried to figure out how to go back to the dance world. Even though I couldn't point my feet, I still identified as a dancer.

It was a long process. I had to change my perception of what a dancer can be. I could still move and express with my body. That set me on the path of exploring possibilities and finding solutions. I had my first experience back in dance through teaching opportunities. I then started choreographing on theater companies. I eventually moved to Melbourne and started applying for funding to support my own work. However, it got to the point in Australia that I felt like a lone crusader. Nobody knew what to do with me, and I still wanted to dance. It just so happened that two friends of mine who had been in New York had taken class at American Ballet Theater, and saw a woman take the whole class using her wheelchair. That person was Kitty Lunn. They told her about me and we started connecting.

Before I knew it, Kitty invited me to come and work with her. In 1999, I travelled to New York City to meet a complete stranger. Kitty opened possibilities and showed me how to translate techniques onto my body. Until then, I hadn't been exposed to anybody else with a disability.

I studied with Kitty in 1999 and went back again in 2001 to choreograph on her company. After that, I travelled to the UK to study

with Candoco Dance Company. I felt welcomed and at home. I joined the company in 2003 and danced with them until 2008.

I wanted more opportunities to choreograph, so I founded Marc Brew Company and started getting commissions, including for dance companies that aren't integrated.

In 2011, I received a commission from AXIS Dance Company. Since then, I've worked with the company on and off, choreographing, touring, and rewriting their summer intensive curriculum. When the artistic director, Judith Smith, decided to retire, she asked me to become the artistic director. I took over the company in January 2017, and Judy officially retired in 2018.

How would you describe your current dance practice?

I stretch every morning, but I would love to be in class more. My focus now is on the dancers in AXIS and what they need. The company rehearses five days a week. I try to be in the studio with them as often as I can, usually every day. It's important for me to teach the company. Working in integrated dance, there's not one way to do a step.

It's also important for me to have my own artistic opportunities as a dancer. I still do projects with other companies. For example, I was recently in Seoul, South Korea doing a collaboration. From there, I went to Australia to work with a dance theater company.

> "It's important for me to claim ownership of my disability. I used to write it out of my bio, but now I claim it: I am a disabled man. I am a gay man. There's nothing to be ashamed of.

When you tell people you are a dancer, what are the most common reactions you receive?

People have assumed I can't speak, just because I'm in a wheelchair. Or, if someone is standing next to me, questions are directed to them, as if I can't communicate. A lot of that is due to unfamiliarity with disability. Having a sense of humor really helps. If someone stares, I stare back or ask if they are okay. I had to learn to be more assertive. Some people are really brash and say, "What do you mean you dance? You're wheelchair bound." I'm not bound to my chair. I don't sleep in my chair or use the toilet from my chair. I've had to become an educator, which gets tiring at times.

When I first would tell people I'm a dancer, they had this look on their faces of, "Oh, this poor guy thinks he's a dancer." Back then, there were physical barriers that prevented people in wheelchairs from even leaving their homes. Thankfully, there's more visibility and awareness, but a lot of places don't have that yet.

Especially in the UK, arts councils have made a point to support artists with disabilities. There are regular funding opportunities available for disabled artists, and not just in dance. In America, we need to find ways to have disability voices heard. When we talk about inclusion, it's focused on race and gender, but disability is left out.

What are some ways people discuss dance with regards to disability that you feel carry problematic implications or assumptions?

A lot of reviewers don't know how to talk about dance and disability. They write about what they see, like the wheelchairs or canes. There's the element of inspirational porn, "Isn't it amazing?!" They forget the other dancers onstage who don't have physical disabilities, so there becomes a disparity in the focus. It becomes about the disability, rather than the art.

There's starting to be a shift. Organizations like Dance/NYC and Dance/USA are educating the dance world. Writers need to learn about disability culture so they can be more informed. Right now, coverage is rooted in description, instead of the intentions driving the work.

Do you believe there are adequate training opportunities for dancers with disabilities? If not, what areas would you specifically like to see improved?

No way! All of us in the field are trying to move that forward. Whether it's a company or university, there are gatekeepers who won't open the doors to dancers with disabilities. If they did, they would benefit from unique perspectives. Institutions need to reflect the world we live in.

I revised AXIS' summer intensive curriculum three years ago. It's now comprised of three different modules. The first is centered on improvisation and site-specific work, which is often the way people with disabilities access dance. The next module focuses on choreography and performance. We look at how to translate dance techniques for people with disabilities, and the participants also learn repertoire and choreography in small groups. The last module is a three-day teacher training. We look at the barriers to access teachers work within and develop tools and proactive ways they can be more inclusive in their practice.

But more needs to be done. We're starting to offer trainings at festivals and with other organizations and companies. Things are moving forward but it's not happening quickly. Those gatekeepers don't want to change the way things have been done for so long, especially in traditional educational institutions.

This year, AXIS initiated our first Choreo-Lab for disabled choreographers. Supporting the next generation of disabled choreographers is a big passion of mine.

Would you like to see disability in dance assimilated into the mainstream?

That's a tricky question. My personal feeling is there are benefits to something like a festival solely focused on supporting artists with disabilities. There's something empowering about coming together to share and learn from each other, because it doesn't happen often. In the UK, the Unlimited Festival brings those artists together, and it's really positive.

But there's also the question of: Do we want to ghettoize dance artists with disabilities? It's about where we place it. Disability dance should be on mainstages and in major festivals. It should be part of the larger dance world, but it is a particular focus. When I was in London, there was a conversation about if general audiences at high profile venues want to see disability dance. I argue that, if anything, it's a different perspective and some audiences are hungry and excited for it.

What is your preferred term for the field?

I very much resonate with the social model of disability where it's not my disability that disables me; it's the social attitudes and environments I live in that disable me. If structures were made accessible, I'd be able to independently access them.

I think "physically integrated dance" is almost too specific a term. AXIS is not only physically integrated, but also integrated in terms of race and gender. I use the term "integrated dance," but my hope is that one day it won't be needed, that we can just be a dance company. However, it's also important for me to claim ownership of my disability. I used to write it out of my bio, but now I claim it: I am a disabled man. I am a gay man. There's nothing to be ashamed of. It's been empowering to be outward about those identities.

In your perspective, is the field improving with time?

I think it is. There's more awareness. Here in the states, there are other disabled artists getting support, but it's just beginning. The focus has been on traditional dance companies like AXIS that have been around for 30 years, but independent dancers and choreographers with disabilities also need support.

Kitty Lunn is a ballet and modern dancer and teacher, a disability activist, and the founder of Infinity Dance Theater, a dance company founded in 1995 featuring dancers with and without disabilities. Based in New York City, Kitty is committed to bringing motion and movement to a new level of inclusion by expanding the boundaries of dance and changing perceptions of what a dancer is. To this end, she has developed wheelchair dance techniques strongly rooted in classical ballet and modern dance.

"I'm Waiting for the World to Catch Up with Me"
This interview was conducted by Emmaly Wiederholt in May 2018

How did you get into dance and what have been some highlights in your dance history?

My grandmother took me to see *The Red Shoes* for my eighth birthday. I looked up at that beautiful red-headed ballerina, and I wanted to be her. I was lucky enough to have lessons. I'm from New Orleans originally, and my teacher was from the Paris Opera Ballet. She recognized something in me and put me on track to become that red-headed ballerina. That's how it all started.

From New Orleans, I went to Washington Ballet. I had the opportunity to work with many famous dancers, including Erik Bruhn, Margot Fonteyn, Rudolf Nureyev, and José Limón. José was my first introduction to modern dance, though I later met Martha Graham.

When I had my accident in 1987, I thought my dancing days were over. I was in the hospital for almost three years. Congress passed the Americans with Disabilities Act in 1990. By 1992, I was ready to go back to dance, and didn't think twice about taking class. I didn't realize at the time that what I was doing was so radical; I was taking regular ballet classes in my wheelchair.

My first class back was on a Saturday at noon at Steps. Vladimir Malakhov and Paloma Herrera were in that class. They made a place for me at the barre. It was wonderful. I knew then that I was going to be okay.

That is not to say everyone was thrilled I was there. They still aren't.

How would you describe your current dance practice?

I take either ballet or modern six days a week. This morning I took a Horton class. I currently rehearse twice a week, though that increases in the summer. Right now, I'm rehearsing at Hunter College. In the summer, there aren't as many classes, so I have more access to the space to teach and rehearse.

I create my work first and then I schedule a show. I don't schedule a show and then force myself to create. This is because of the dancers I work with. I often have to train them from scratch. This is especially true of those in power chairs. I never put someone onstage just because they have a disability. The training process can take months. When the piece is ready or near completion, I think about where we will perform it.

A lot of theaters in New York are not wheelchair accessible. This is also a problem with touring. I used to travel five times a year, but it's difficult with power chairs and manual chairs. I don't travel as much anymore. I'm going to be 70 soon. I'm at an age and station where I do the work I want with the dancers I choose.

When you tell people you are a dancer, what are the most common reactions you receive?

People assume that I used to be a dancer. I used to get that a lot. I don't get that as much anymore because I'm pretty well-known in the circles I travel in.

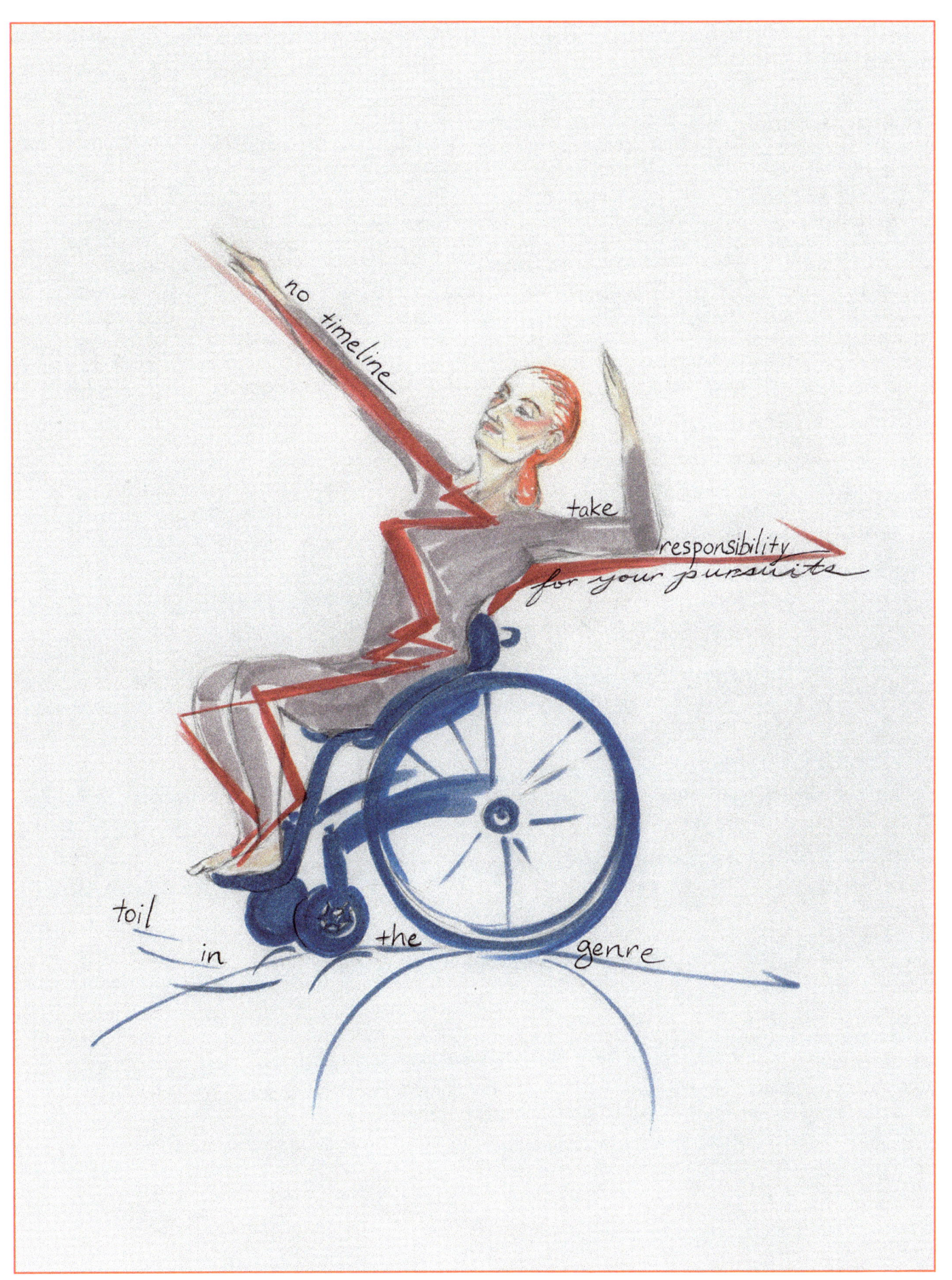

What are some ways people discuss dance with regards to disability that you feel carry problematic implications or assumptions?

People get really hung up on the happy cripple thing and how courageous and brave I am. It takes a while to get to the art. In interviews, I tell people that my accident was an accident; what I do now is a choice. If you find it inspirational, fine, but let's talk about the art. Those of us who toil in this genre, we don't look at what we're doing as brave and courageous. I think some of the topics I have covered are brave and courageous. I'm a risk-taker that way. But there are always going to be those who are amazed I breathe, dress, and feed myself.

I am not a disability rights in-your-face kind of an activist. I have always let my work speak for itself. I don't consider my disability as the paramount thing in my life. I describe myself as a woman who is an artist – and by that I mean dancer and choreographer – with a disability. It's not that I don't refer to myself as a disabled person, but there's so much more to me than my disability.

I don't make dances about disability. My disability informs every aspect of my life; I don't put my disability away when I go to sleep at night, and I'm still disabled when I get up in the morning. I don't make dances about disability, but the fact that I'm doing what I'm doing, some would consider me politically active. I don't think about my disability until I'm facing a bunch of stairs and there's no way for me to get in. Or if I really need to go to the bathroom and there's no place for me to go. It's not that I'm trying to not be disabled, my disability just is. It's neither good nor bad. I don't think of it as a negative unless there's something I want to do, and there's no way for me to do it.

As far as press, there are still many mainstream dance folks who do not think what I do is dance. I don't care. If someone's outlook is so narrow they can't get past the fact that different bodies move differently, that's their problem.

In my lifetime, theaters were shut down because there were mixed races dancing together. New York City Ballet was ticketed because Arthur Mitchell was dancing with Tanny Le Clercq. People were incensed that a Black man was partnering a white woman. I think the solution to the problem is to get out there and make the work that matters, regardless.

> "Who I am is a dancer, so I had to find a way to keep dancing. That is who Kitty Lunn is. I'm waiting for the world to catch up with me.

Do you believe there are adequate training opportunities for dancers with disabilities? If not, what areas would you specifically like to see improved?

I didn't realize it was radical when I went back to class. They had to let me in because the ADA said so. Twenty-five years ago, I thought by now there would be 25 of me, but there aren't, and that makes me sad. It's not that my way is the only way. My way is a way that has worked very successfully for me and my students.

There's a whole philosophy, particularly on the West Coast, that if you do contact improvisation, you don't need technique. I disagree. When Prince Siegfried lifts Odile in Swan Lake, that's weight sharing and counterbalance. I use a lot of contact improvisation in the rehearsal process, but after a while, it no longer becomes improvisation. We keep some things and throw out other things.

My choreography looks different on every body. I like that. It makes the process very dynamic but can also make it slow. Disability is not tube socks; it's not one size fits all. I happen to have a spinal cord injury. Even with spinal cord injuries, each one is different. I have several dancers with cerebral palsy and each is different. I'm interested in those differences.

When I train my students, it's not that I believe my class is the be-all-and-end-all. I'm trying to give them enough basic technique and confidence that they'll take the risk of putting themselves in a mainstream class.

That's how it's going to change. It's not going to change by constantly segregating ourselves. Believe me, there are many more non-disabled dancers than disabled dancers. I tell people all the time: "If you want to be a dancer, go where the dancers are. If it's an open class, they can't not let you in. But you have to grow a thick skin."

Would you like to see disability in dance assimilated into the mainstream?

I would, yes. I would love that. We can reach more audiences that way. When we start seeing dancers with disabilities guesting with Mark Morris or New York City Ballet, that's what's going to change things. But I don't think it's going to happen in my lifetime. I'm not saying that Infinity Dance Theater can't hold an audience on its own – we certainly have for almost 25 years. However, dancing is a choice. It's not an entitlement. I started dancing when I was eight. Most dancers with disabilities come to it later in life. That's okay, but they have catching up to do. The disability community is not willing to take a lot of risks in terms of putting themselves in a mainstream position. If you live somewhere like New York City where there's dance going on practically everywhere, then go put your money down and put yourself in a class. I understand it's frightening. Dance is tough. But if you're waiting for someone to welcome you, not everyone will. Misty Copeland didn't become a principal dancer with ABT because she is Black. In many ways, she became a principal dancer in spite of being Black. I get a little frustrated when people believe they need special considerations.

I would say the same thing to a person who is non-binary or African American. Who is stopping you from dancing? I do a lot of public speaking on this issue. We have to take responsibility for our own pursuits. God help us if we ever truly get the full promise of the ADA, because then people will have to stop complaining and go to work. If you want to work, go do your work.

What is your preferred term for the field?

I hate the term "special needs" with a passion. I would prefer we get rid of cutesy terminology like "special needs" or "temporarily able-bodied" or "special abilities."

I would rather be just a dancer. If it must be some label though, I would call it "disability dance artistry." I'm on the taskforce at Dance/NYC, and that is our collective preferred term. I don't mind being called a dancer with a disability, but I look forward to the day when I can just be a dancer.

In your perspective, is the field improving with time?

I've been around long enough to see that yes, there has been change. I also know that in some areas a lot has not changed. There are times when I think it was better 10 or 15 years ago. I live in New York City, which isn't a very accessible place. Some subways have elevators, but a lot of times they don't work. Those kinds of hassles that wouldn't necessarily make or break your day make or break my day.

I look at the work I do and the students whom I have influenced, and I'm pleased with the state of the art. What I'm not pleased with is the feeling that disabled dancers don't need to learn how to dance.

Any other thoughts?

I get a lot of criticism. There are many even in the disability community who think I'm an assimilationist. But I needed to get back into dance class. I was a dancer when I became disabled. I tried to stop dancing. It almost killed me. I was not successful in my suicide attempt. Who I am is a dancer, so I had to find a way to keep dancing. That is who Kitty Lunn is. I'm waiting for the world to catch up with me.

SIDIKI CONDE

Sidiki Conde *is originally from Guinea, West Africa, and was severely paralyzed by polio when he was 14. When it came time for the ceremony in which young men dance into manhood, he knew that if he did not participate, he would remain forever cut off from his community. He reconstructed the traditional steps by dancing on his hands. After joining Ballet Les Merveilles de Guinée and touring West Africa, Sidiki's talents brought him to the United States where he founded the Tokounou All-Abilities Dance and Music Ensemble. He continues to live in New York City with his wife.*

"Dance Is About Happiness"

This interview was conducted by Emmaly Wiederholt in April 2019

How did you get into dance and what have been some highlights in your dance history?

I'm from Guinea, West Africa. I was born on March 25th, 1961. When I was 14 years old, I got polio. I was paralyzed. That time was so hard. My father sent me to a village in the forest to live with my grandfather. One day I saw the people doing a ceremony and dancing. They looked happy. Watching them, I forgot my disability and was happy too. After that, I started to study the music and dance. My two brothers helped me. I started training with them. I learned how to stand up on my two hands. I pumped a lot to get the strength. I started to move my knees above my hands because I realized it didn't work to have both my knees and hands on the ground. I lifted my legs up to just dance on my two hands. The people were happy when they saw what I was doing. They pushed me to keep going. I did the traditional dance for the formal manhood ceremony. It filled me with happiness to join in the dancing.

After that, I danced in a small festival before joining Ballet Les Merveilles de Guinée, where I danced for six or seven years. That's where I was trained in all the West African dance forms. During the Guinea-Bissau War, I had a chance to come to the United States. That was in 1998. I've stayed since then.

Coming to New York City was the first time I'd been to such a big city with so many people. At first, I was unsure of my dancing. But when I performed at Lincoln Center, everybody loved it. Now I teach at schools, sharing with the kids and with everybody my story.

How would you describe your current dance practice?

My group is called the Tokounou All-Abilities Dance and Music Ensemble, and we're in New York City. We practice twice a week. I work with the traditional music and dance steps. We do a lot of school shows to teach children how to do the dances and songs. I just taught four classes this morning at a school in Long Island.

When you tell people you are a dancer, what are the most common reactions you receive?

People are surprised. They wonder how I dance. If I say that I'm a dancer, people ask, "How?" And when they see me dance, they can't believe it. They don't know how it can be. It was the same reaction in Guinea as it is in the United States.

What are some ways people discuss dance with regards to disability that you feel carry problematic implications or assumptions?

Every show I do, people are happy to watch, and I'm happy to dance. I never think about having a disability. I just think about dancing.

Everybody can dance, even without using legs, like in my case. Dance is about happiness, and everybody needs happiness. I am disabled, it's true. But at the end of the day, dance is dance. Dance imitates the animals or nature through movement, and doing those movements brings happiness.

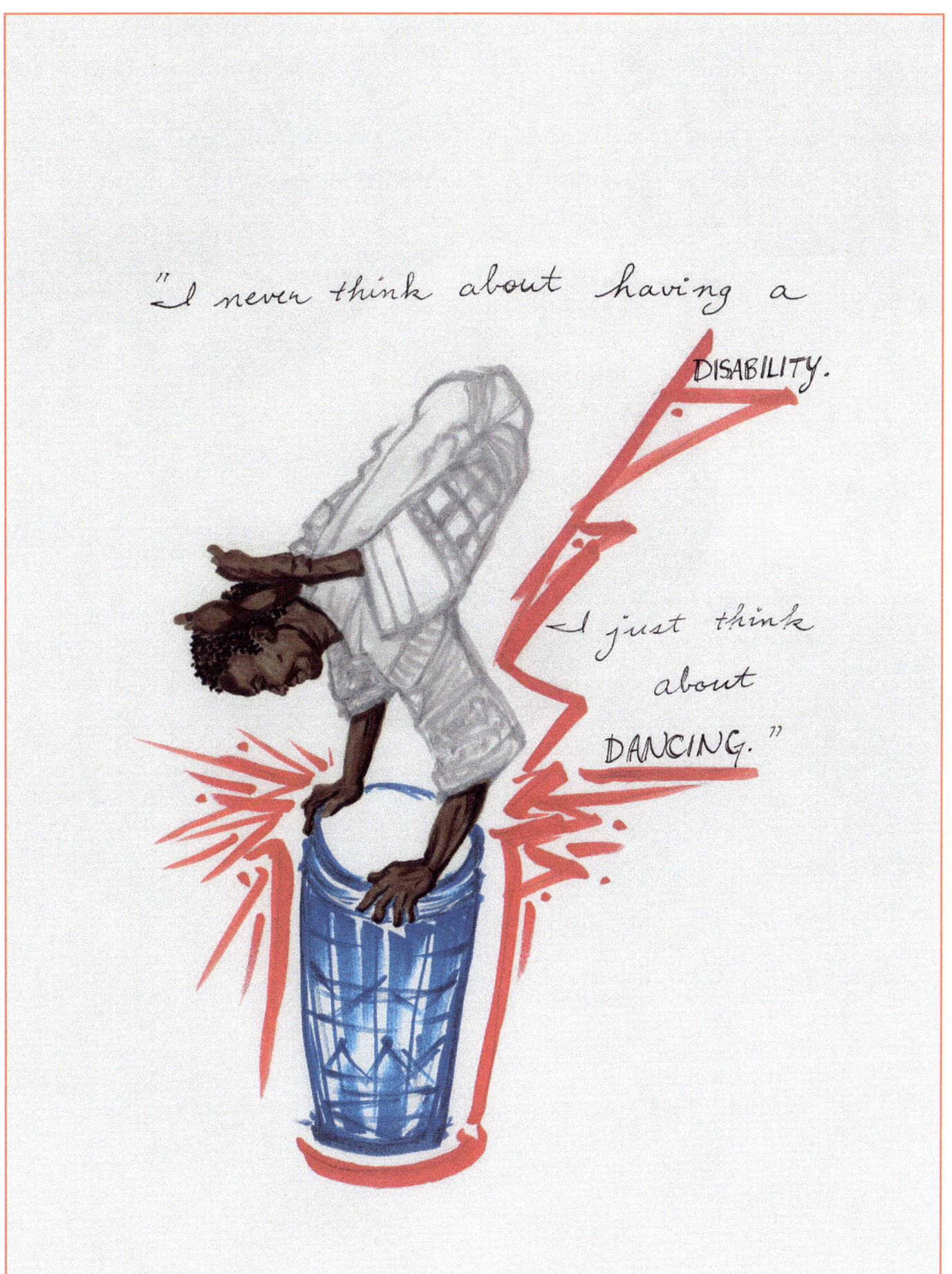

Do you believe there are adequate training opportunities for dancers with disabilities?

I believe in teaching kids to dance, absolutely, including those with disabilities. That's why I do it myself. But I'd like there to be more of it in the schools.

Would you like to see disability in dance assimilated into the mainstream?

That would be great. I think a festival focusing on disability is great, but I want to be able to dance in any festival in the world.

> "Everybody can dance, even without using legs, like in my case. Dance is about happiness, and everybody needs happiness. I am disabled, it's true. But at the end of the day, dance is dance.

What is your preferred term for the field?

In my country, I was the only disabled dancer. All the other dancers danced normally with their feet; I was the only one dancing on my hands. But I never thought of myself as having a disability, I just danced differently. If you work hard, you can dance.

In your perspective, is the field improving with time?

Of course. That's my goal and my dream, to make life better for all of us. You have to work hard though. Depend on yourself, not on others. Before you get help, you must help yourself first.

Any other thoughts?

Have courage and faith. Have courage to do exactly what you want to do. Find your happiness. Happiness comes from the movement in dance, and everybody can move. Maybe you're playing the drums or dancing, but there's always something you can do. That's my main message.

Sidiki Conde

COLLABORATOR BIOGRAPHIES

Emmaly Wiederholt is a dance artist and arts journalist based in Albuquerque, New Mexico. She is the founder and editor of Stance on Dance (stanceondance.com), a dance journalism nonprofit that dissects the dance world. Emmaly earned her MA in arts journalism from the University of Southern California and her BFA in ballet and BS in political science from the University of Utah. She further trained at the San Francisco Conservatory of Dance and performed extensively around the Bay Area. Her first book, *Beauty is Experience: Dancing 50 and Beyond*, was published in 2017. She continues to perform and teach throughout the Southwest.

Silva Laukkanen loves the beautiful moments that are created in space by bodies telling stories. During a chance opportunity to teach at a rehabilitation center in her native Finland, she was reminded of the transformative power of movement in the lives of everyday people, and because of this experience she decided to focus her career on community and inclusive dance. She wants to expand the notion of who can dance and where dance should happen. This inquiry sparked the idea in 2016 to start DanceCast: a podcast to bring awareness about dance artists working outside traditional norms.

Liz Brent-Maldonado is a multi-disciplinary creator of art, writing, and holistic educational experiences. Originally from Colorado, she is a University of Colorado at Boulder alum and lived in Kyoto, Japan before moving to San Francisco in 2009. Liz loves design, research, travel, colors, and coffee. Whether costumes or comics, her favorite projects feature magical realism and the everyday infused with otherworldly or surreal elements. She delights in the intersections of the practical and theatrical, the fantastical and the scientific, movement and stillness, comfort and organization, solitary focus with team collaboration. For more, visit www.sparkle.vision.

Christelle Dreyer is a dancer and graphic designer in Cape Town, South Africa. She obtained her Bachelor of Technology in Graphic Design in 2011 from the Cape Peninsula University of Technology and is currently working towards her master's degree in Graphic Design. She has studied ballroom and Latin dance styles and has won numerous ballroom dance championship titles. Through Remix Dance Project, Christelle has taught dance to schoolchildren. In 2017, she received the Cultural Affairs Award from the Western Cape Government for Contribution by Person with Disability to The Arts.

Donne "the Wychdokta" Lewis is a percussive dance artist, musician, writer, editor, and communications professional.

April Adams is a social justice advocate with a background in creative placemaking, community engagement, organizational management, and art program administration.

Sami Kekäläinen is a musician and a curious being based in Helsinki, Finland. Among his various endeavours, he produces electronic music, raps, and performs as a street musician. As well as being passionate about the arts, he's also a bit of a science geek with interests in psychology, neuroscience and biology. He is also interested in the world of dance and movement and inspired by it, and has composed the music for the Kaaos Company performance *Mirage* in 2021.

OUR MOST SINCERE THANKS TO THESE AND MANY OTHERS WHO HELPED MAKE THIS BOOK POSSIBLE

Geral Alessi
Jeremy Alliger
Satsuki Annino
Meghan Armstrong
Maylis Arrabit
Nancy S. Bain
Iris Bouche
Frances Brent
Greg Brent
Marc Brew
Debra Cash
Monique Chantal
Bradford Chin
Stephanie Clemens
Devan Conness
Karen Daly
Trevor Davis
Sarah Delafuente
Kristina Dickson
Ann DiFruscia
Sydney Erlikh
Mina Estrada
Elyse Fahey
Kyle Farrell
Sonja Franeta
Elise Gent
Alex Gill
James Graham
Jason Wadsworth
Sonya Green

Esther Grimm
Narissa Guba
Rena Marie Guidry
Amanda Hamp
Kathryn Harden
Yolanda Head
Matthew Henley
Paul Herndon
Potter and Terry Herndon
Lorien House
Lisa Hueske
Renee Infelise
Cathy Intemann
Nick Ishimaru
Emily Jones
Monica Keegan
Dan Knox
Michaela Knox
Karenne H Koo
Eric Kupers
Sandra Kurtz
Paul Langland
Kristine Larsen
Heidi Latsky
Kelcie Laube
Sharon Laube
Pentti Laukkanen
Malinda LaVelle
Sara Lawrence-Sucato

Bonnie Lewkowicz
Sandra Paola Lopez Ramirez
Charles Lowell
Victoria Marks
Samantha Martinez
Barbara McAlister
Jennifer Meerpohl
Susan Myers
Emily Navarra
Jennifer Norris
Jessie Nowak
Julie Noyes
Michael Paap
Tim Page
Monica Parra
Ellice Patterson
Amanda Perez
Sofia Puchner
Fran Quinlan
Olivia Raynor
Mark Robinson
Allan and Vicki Rodrigues
Arun Rodrigues
Kamala Rodrigues
Elizabeth Rosenberg
Lizett Ross
Heather Rudow
Carrie Sandahl

Douglas Scott
Lara Segura
Andrew Seiler
Lauren Sheely
Stephanie Simpson
Danae Sims
Sara Slawnik
Judith Smith
Leea Sokura
Spank Dance
Maggie Stack
Sandra Stratton-Gonzalez
Timo Taskinen
Mark Tomasic
Connie Vandarakis
Ronja Ver
Mariah W
Jenny Walker
Amy Weinkauf
David Wiederholt
Katie Wiederholt
Martin Wiederholt
Martha Williamson
Clemency Wings
Elizabeth Winkelaar
Rachelle Woods
Matthew Wycislak
Ching Chi Yu